Women in the
Middle Ages

Women in the Middle Ages
Religion, Marriage and Letters

ANGELA M. LUCAS

*Lecturer in English, St Patrick's College,
Maynooth, Ireland*

ST. MARTIN'S PRESS
NEW YORK

For information, write:
St. Martin's Press, Inc., 175 Fifth Avenue, New York, NY 10010
Printed in Great Britain
First published in the United States of America in 1983

Library of Congress Card Catalog Number: 82-42578

ISBN 0-312-88743-4

For Peter

A wyf sholde eek be mesurable in looking and in berynge and in lawghyng, and discreet in alle hire wordes and hire dedes.

Contents

Preface

———◆———

Woman's place in society is a subject which has enjoyed much
discussion in recent years. To relate woman's role in literature
to ideas prevailing in the society for which that literature was
written seems an obvious dimension to explore, and several
explorations of attitudes to women found in medieval English
literature have been made. The scope of this book is limited to
three areas, Religion, Marriage and Letters, and my interest in
the English woman in the Middle Ages (a term which for me
also includes the period called by historians the 'dark ages')
determines the geographical range of the book: English women
are at the centre of discussion, but from time to time I refer also
to women in continental Europe.

Those living in the Middle Ages lacked our modern concept
'literature', and so the word 'literature' has been interpreted to
include not only works of generally recognized literary merit,
but also wills and charters, theological, philosophical and
medical treatises, as well as sermons and homilies which relate
to women. The effect is thus cross-disciplinary, but the basis
lies in my teaching of Old and Middle English literature. Some
of the works are of a serious and factual nature, others overtly
fictional, yet even most fiction in the Middle Ages was not
without a didactic function. It is necessary also to state by way
of caution that most of the information we have about women in
the Middle Ages was written down by men, and that a great
deal of that information relates to women of the upper or upper
middle classes.

Chronologically, the investigations in the three areas do not generally extend later than the fifteenth century on the one hand, or earlier than the fifth on the other, except in the case of patristic and other texts illustrative of the common Christian heritage of Western Europe. Where quotations are used they are intended to illustrate the relevant matters under discussion. The Middle Ages provide many varieties of opinion about women and I have sometimes illustrated such disparate views and allowed the material to speak for itself without undue comment.

Where modern language translations of Latin works are available these have been referred to or cited, otherwise references are to Latin texts with assistance in translation as acknowledged below. Texts and editions have been generally chosen for quality and accessibility. I owe a debt of gratitude to those who have worked in this field before me. I have attempted to acknowledge their influence either in the text or in the Select Bibliography or both. Unfortunately, Régine Pernoud's book *La Femme au Temps des Cathédrales* came to my attention too late to be an influence. Readers wishing to follow up references in the text should consult the first page of the Select Bibliography, where divisions used in the Bibliography and the method of referring to sources are explained.

I have pleasure in thanking all those who have helped me in the preparation of the book: St Patrick's College, Maynooth, for granting me sabbatical leave in which to complete the work; the Maynooth Scholastic Trust for a grant towards the expense of preparing the book for publication; the secretarial staff at Maynooth, especially Mrs Maureen Redmond and Miss Mary Murphy; Dr Graham Anderson, Department of Classics, The University of Kent at Canterbury; Dr Raymond Astbury, Department of Classics, University College Dublin; Mrs Mary Cullen, Department of History, St Patrick's College Maynooth; Mr Alan Fletcher, Department of Old and Middle English, University College Dublin; Dr Joseph Long, Department of French, University College Dublin; Miss Evelyn Mullally, Department of French, The Queen's University of Belfast;

Miss Ann Crowley, Department of Adult Education, St Patrick's College Maynooth; Rev. Christopher O'Donnell, O. Carm.; Mrs Ann Coogan, who typed the greater part of the manuscript; Mr Robert Baldock, formerly of The Harvester Press Ltd., and the staff at Harvester; Cambridge University Library for the unwavering courtesy of its staff. My thanks are also due to the National University of Ireland for a grant-in-aid towards the cost of publication. My deepest gratitude, however, goes to my husband, to whom the book is dedicated; a fellow medievalist, he bore patiently with me through all stages of the book's preparation, and his encouragement and constructive criticism sustained me through to its conclusion.

Angela M. Lucas

St Patrick's College, Maynooth
Feast of the Immaculate Conception, 1981

List of Abbreviations

———◆———

Abbreviated bibliographical references are also to be found in square brackets at the end of the relevant entries in the Select Bibliography (p. 189).

AN	Anglo–Norman
ACW	Ancient Christian Writers, Westminster, Maryland (1946–)
AS	Anglo-Saxon
ASC	Anglo-Saxon Chronicle
ASPR	Anglo-Saxon Poetic Records, ed. G. P. Krapp and E. v. K. Dobbie, New York and London (1931–53)
BJRL	*Bulletin of the John Ryland's Library*
CCSL	Corpus Christianorum Series Latina, Turnhout
CCCM	Corpus Christianorum continuatio Medievalis, Turnhout
CCM	*Cahiers de Civilisation Médiévale*
EETS	Early English Text Society, Original Series
EETS (ES)	Early English Text Society, Extra Series
EETS (SS)	Early English Text Society, Supplementary Series
EHD	English Historical Documents
EHR	*English Historical Review*
ES	*English Studies*
FC	Fathers of the Church, New York (1947)
ME	Middle English
MGH	Monumenta Germaniae Historica

MLR	*Modern Language Review*
MP	*Modern Philology*
MS	*Mediaeval Studies*
NPNF	A Select Library of the Nicene and Post-Nicene Fathers of the Christian Church, New York (First Series 1886–92, Second Series 1890–1900)
OE	Old English
OF	Old French
PL	Patrologia cursus completus, series Latina, Paris (1844–55)
RB	*Revue Bénédictine*
RS	Rolls Series; Chronicles and Memorials of Great Britain and Ireland during the Middle Ages, London (1858–)
SC	Sources Chrétiennes, Paris (1941–)
SATF	Société des Anciens Textes Français, Paris (1875–)
SCH	Studies in Church History
SSP	Surtees Society Publications
TRHS	*Transactions of the Royal Historical Society*
TAPS	*Transactions of the American Philosophical Society*

Part One

Women and Religion

I

For Mannes Helpe y-Wroght?

<hr />

Woman is first mentioned in the Bible in Gen. 1:26–7:

> Then God said, 'Let us make man in our image, after our likeness. . . .'
> So God created man in his own image, in the image of God he created him; male and female he created them.

In Gen. 2:21–3 we are told more:

> So the Lord God caused a deep sleep to fall upon the man, and while he slept took one of his ribs and closed up its place with flesh; and the rib which the Lord God had taken from the man he made into a woman and brought her to the man.
> Then the man said,
>
> > 'This at last is bone of my bones
> > and flesh of my flesh;
> > she shall be called Woman,
> > because she was taken out of
> > man.'

These verses in the Book of Genesis, and the subsequent narrative of Temptation and Fall, to which may be added certain statements found in the Epistles of St Paul, may be seen as of paramount importance in the development of moral attitudes to women by theologians and philosophers. Interpretations of these texts by scriptural commentators have tended towards an unfavourable view of woman and it was with the aid of the biblical commentaries on Genesis by the Church Fathers, that the churchmen of the Middle Ages formulated their views. They drew especially on the works of Augustine

3

and Ambrose, and reproduced the same ideas repeatedly in their own exegetical and other works. Gen. 1:26 gave rise to questions about the two terms 'image' and 'likeness'. Are they to be considered analogous or is some distinction to be made between them? Is woman made in God's image, as is Adam, or is she only made in His likeness? Some writers did not admit that woman was made directly in the image of God, but argued rather that she was made in the image of Adam, because she was created from his side.

Gen. 1:26–7 allowed for the understanding that 'man' meant both male and female: '. . . in the image of God he created him; male and female he created them'. The notion that God created man as an idea, a type, neither male nor female, by nature incorruptible, was put forward by Philo of Alexandria in the first century after Christ (Philo of Alexandria, *De Op. Mundi*, 134), and though it did not receive wide currency in the Middle Ages, some echoes of it are to be found. Gregory of Nyssa (330–95) believed that sexuality was the result of original sin (Gregory of Nyssa, *De Hom. Op.*, xvii). John Scotus Eriugena, ninth-century translator of Gregory, maintained that in the final *apocatastasis* the distinction between the sexes would disappear (Eriugena, *Periphiseon*, v). Ernaud, a twelfth-century abbot of Bonneval near Chartres, also maintained that at the end of time there would no longer be male and female, but one complete and perfect creature (Ernaud of Bonneval, *Hex.*, 1534). He also developed at great length a comparison between the sexes whereby man stands for the higher rational soul, often called *mens* or *spiritus*, whereas woman stands for *anima* the lower rational soul, or *sensus* the sensible, even sensual, part of humanity.

This opposition of flesh and spirit, sensuality and reason, is found in Philo of Alexandria (*Legum*, II, 24; II, 35–9) and by the twelfth century it was more or less commonplace. It had been found much earlier in both Ambrose (*De Par.*, xi, 53; *Hex.*, VI, vii, 40), and Augustine (*De Gen. Contra Man.*, II, xi). Woman is fully human, a creature of God, spiritually man's

4

equal, yet her spirituality is more earthy, and more closely allied to the sensual. If man and woman are to each other as intelligence is to sensibility, then the subjection of woman to man is to be regarded as proper and natural, for reason governs the senses and the soul governs the body.

Isidore of Seville (c.560–636) linked the terms for male and female to strength and frailty by indulging in a little word play. The Latin word *vir*, he says, is related to *vis*, meaning strength, and *mulier* is related to *mollitie*, meaning softness or weakness (Isidore of Seville, *Etym.*, XI, ii, 17–18). Alan of Lille in the twelfth century arrives at a similar conclusion (Alan of Lille, *Distinct.*, 865). For Abelard the word *mulier* indicated a deficiency of the spirit and a deprivation of discernment, whilst man by contrast was distinguished by his firmness of reason and spirit (Abelard, *Hex.*, 760–1). Peter Abelard also believed that man had more wisdom and reason than a woman. One of the most influential of twelfth-century theologians, Hugh of St Victor, departed from this Philonian notion by establishing a threefold comparison: first, wisdom, which is reason turned towards things divine; second, prudence, which is reason turned towards things human; third, sensibility which is a desire for earthly things. Man is thus the image of wisdom, woman of prudence, and the beast the image of sensibility or sensuality. However, Hugh was careful to make it clear that he is only making a comparison and that all three faculties co-exist in every human being (Hugh of St Victor, *De Sac. Ch. Fid.*, I, viii, 13). This seems to be a most fair conclusion, for even if man is acknowledged as superior to woman by virtue of his wisdom, yet intelligence and sensibility are indispensable to one another and must co-exist, and so must male and female.

Augustine had admitted that 'Human nature itself which is complete [only] in both sexes, was made in the image of God, and it does not separate the woman from the image of God which it signifies. . . . The woman together with her own husband is the image of God, so that the whole may be one image' (Augustine of Hippo, *De Trinitate*, vii). However, he goes

5

on to make it clear that while man alone is in the image of God as fully as when joined to woman, woman alone is not to be regarded as in God's image. St Thomas Aquinas was equally firm:

> The image of God in its principal signification, namely the intellectual nature, is found both in man and in woman. Hence, after the words *To the image of God he created him*, it is added *Male and female he created them* in the plural, as Augustine (*Gen. ad lit.* iii, 22) remarks, lest it should be thought that both sexes were united in one individual. But in a secondary sense the image of God is found in man, and not in woman: for man is the beginning and end of woman; as God is the beginning and end of every creature. So when the apostle had said that *man is the image and glory of God, but woman is the glory of man*, he adds his reason for saying this: for man is not of woman but woman of man; and man was not created for woman, but woman for man. (Thomas Aquinas, *Summa*, pt.I, q.XCIII, art.4)

Isidore of Seville believed that woman, formed specially from man's side, is in the image of man, whilst man is in the image of God, and thus woman must naturally submit to man (Isidore of Seville, *Sent.*, I, xi, 4–6). In the twelfth century, Gratian, the 'father' of Canon Law, indicated that woman was not made in God's image, the natural result of which is her subjection to man, the lesser serving the greater, without authority, unable to teach, witness or govern (Gratian, *Decretum*, cols 1254–5). The line of descent from St Paul is very clear: 'I permit no woman to teach or to have authority over men; she is to keep silent. For Adam was formed first, then Eve' (1 Tim. 2:12–13). Scholars like Abelard and Ernaud followed this line; Rupert of Deutz, contemporary of Abelard, produced the variant that woman *was* in the image of God before the Fall, but subjection to man is one of her punishments for original sin (Rupert of Deutz, *In Genesim*, II, 7, pp. 191ff). This view is also found in the work of Andrew of St Victor (d'Alverny, 1977, p. 112). Thomas Aquinas' view was that the order of creation reinforced the notion of man's superiority over woman, paralleling man's creativity in relation to the human race with God's in relation to the whole universe.

> When all things were first formed, it was more suitable for the woman to be made from the man than . . . [as happens] in other animals. Firstly, in order thus to give the first man a certain dignity consisting in this, that as God is the principle of the whole universe, so the first man, in likeness to God, was the principle of the whole human race. . . . Secondly, that man might love woman all the more and cleave to her more closely, knowing her to be fashioned from himself. (Thomas Aquinas, *Summa*, pt.I, q.XCII, art.2)

The description of the formation of Eve from Adam's side was given different levels of interpretation. One interpretation is that referred to by St Thomas Aquinas in his second reason for the order of creation first quoted above – the union of man and woman was instituted by God in Paradise when He created Eve. Woman formed from man's side was a sign of conjugal love. But the creation of woman was capable of mystical interpretation, as a sacred symbol prefiguring the birth of the Church from the wounded side of the dying Christ. This mystical interpretation of Eve as the Church was much cited in the Middle Ages, following St Augustine (*In Joannis Evang. tract.*, X, ii) and St Ambrose (*De Par.*, xiv, 72) and often quoting St Paul:

> For the husband is head of the wife as Christ is of the Church. . . . Husbands, love your wives, as Christ loved the Church and gave himself up for her. . . . For this reason a man shall leave his father and mother and be joined to his wife and the two shall become one flesh. This mystery is a profound one and I am saying that it refers to Christ and the Church. (Eph. 5:23, 25, 31–2)

For Ambrose (*De. Par.*, ix) woman was made to propagate the species; for Isidore (*Sent.*, I, xi, 4–6) she was made in order to help man, yet he, like Paul, recalls man's duty towards woman: man must set her an example, not expect her to be more virtuous than she is able (Isidore of Seville, *De Eccles. officiis*, II, xx, 13). Her childbearing was seen by commentators like Peter the Chanter (d'Alverny, 1977, p. 114) and Rupert of Deutz (*In Genesim*, III, 21–2) as one of her punishments for transgression, yet children had been seen as a means of salvation by St Paul after her great misdemeanour: 'Yet woman will be saved through bearing children if she continues in faith and love and holiness with modesty' (1 Tim. 2:15). Taking its inspiration from St Augustine, the Middle Ages fostered the notion that woman was made from man's side to indicate that she is to be his companion, more dear to him than any other because she is of his flesh. Hugh of St Victor, one of the most influential of twelfth-century theologians developed the idea thus: she was not created from man's head and so is not meant to be his mistress; she was not created from his feet, and so is not meant to be a slave (Hugh of St Victor, *De. Sac. Ch. Fid.*, I, vi, 35–6). Upon this topos could be built an approach to marriage based on voluntary and reciprocal love. A woman's submission to her husband had to be free, and the husband had to treat her with love and care. As Thomas Aquinas said, she must submit 'that man might love woman all the more and cleave to her more closely'.

According to Ambrose, Eve had to turn to her husband and serve him, and allow herself to be governed by him, after she had repented of her sin (Ambrose, *De Par.*, xiv, 72). Like St Paul, Ambrose goes on to compare this relationship with the pious servitude of the Church to Christ. Woman's submission to man was seen by some as according to the law of nature – as the senses submit to reason, so woman to man. Others put forward the idea that woman was naturally man's equal but as a result of the Fall she is under man's yoke and governance. Isidore's play on words for strength and weakness indicates his view clearly enough. Woman is made in man's image, as a help to him, and so must submit to him. Such a view was reinforced by Roman Law, under which a woman was a perpetual minor, subject first to father or guardian and then to her husband.

Alan of Lille, in the twelfth century, believed in the characteristic weakness of women, feeble in spirit and incapable of firm judgement (d'Alverny, 1977, pp. 113–4), and Abelard too, believing woman to be made only in God's likeness, mentioned that it was woman's basic weakness and inferiority which allowed her to submit to temptation. Thus she is naturally man's inferior, and has to be ruled by him. Abelard generously admits that woman possesses reason and an immortal soul, but still believes that man has more wisdom and reason, and thus is more equal than woman (Abelard, *Hex.*, 76off.).

A timid supporter of woman's equality with man was found in the twelfth century in Andrew of St Victor. Certainly woman's subjection to man was a punishment, but had she not sinned she would have been man's equal (d'Alverny, 1977, p. 112). For Peter the Chanter, woman's submission was a punishment. But he also indicated that before the Fall she would have submitted in love, whereas after it she submitted in fear (d'Alverny, 1977, p. 114).

There was some tension, then, between the spiritual equality of man and woman and the subjection of woman according to social custom. St Paul, so insistent on the headship of husband over wife, can still write: 'There is neither Jew nor Greek, there is neither slave nor free, there is neither male nor female; for you are all one in Christ Jesus' (Gal. 3:28).

Interpretations of the Fall and the apportionment of blame arising from it must take great responsibility for the enormous weight of guilt borne by the descendants of Eve. St Ambrose drew attention to the singular fact that Eve was made within Paradise, Adam outside it, but nevertheless Adam was able to show himself superior to his companion. This female creature made for Paradise was, ironically for Ambrose, the origin of evil and lies (Ambrose, *De Par.*, x, 46–7), and had been responsible for man's fault. For St Paul also, Eve had been deceived, not Adam: 'And Adam was not deceived, but the woman was deceived and became a transgressor' (1 Tim. 2:14). This view was also held by St Jerome, who expounded it with all the energy of a satirist. In spite of being surrounded by women friends, pious Roman ladies whom he truly admired, Jerome could be unwaveringly severe on womankind itself in urgent defence of his celibate state. Woman, he claimed, is the origin of all evils, and it was through her that death entered the world. Woman captures the precious souls and hearts of men, leading them where she will. Woman tends towards pleasure and not virtue, and so is ever a prime instrument in bringing about man's downfall. His text in this case was Ecclesiastes, and so he can use biblical authority to instance woman's lack of virtue: 'One man among a thousand I found, but a woman among all these I have not found' (Eccles. 7:28). He does not scruple to cite Virgil (*Aeneid*, IV, 569–70) in his support: *Varium et mutabile semper Femina* (Jerome, *In Eccles.*, vii). Isidore of Seville produces some more word-play on the name of Eve which indicates his point of view:

'Heva interpretatur "vita", sive calamitas, sive "vae"; *Vita* quia origo fuit nascendi; *calamitas* et *vae*, quia per prevaricationem causa exstitit moriendi'. (Isidore of Seville, *Etym.*, VII, vi, 5)

(Eve means 'life' or 'disaster' or 'woe' – life because she was the origin of being born; disaster or woe because through transgression she became the cause of dying.)

The name is applied to woman in general because she is a cause of both good and misfortune to man. Peter the Chanter saw the Fall in terms of the two sins of woman. Because she succumbed to pride, she is punished by having to submit to man's domination; because she ate the forbidden fruit she is punished in the fruit she will bear (d'Alverny, 1977, p. 114). Adam of Courlandon, a canon of Laon, writing in the early thirteenth century, reasoned that Eve had to be tempted first because she was weaker than Adam. Sense is weaker than reason, and sin begins with the senses. Had Adam been approached first he would have repelled the attack through the power of his reason (d'Alverny, 1977, p. 114).

There are two interesting vernacular treatments of the Fall, one in an Old English poem dating from c.900, and one in Anglo-Norman dating from the twelfth century, which take up this idea: Adam is presented as being tempted first and resisting. The authors of these two literary works are unusual, however, in that they seem less preoccupied with a theological point of view than with the more 'realistic' human question of how it came about that Adam and Eve could be persuaded to break the commandment of God. There could be a tendency to feel that the poet of the OE *Genesis* and the dramatist of the AN *Mystère d'Adam* are moving in the direction of white-washing Eve's part in the Fall, because she does not appear to be approached first by a serpent. In the OE poem *Genesis*, in those lines on the Fall of Man which are known as *Genesis B* because descended from an Old Saxon original, it is explicitly stated that the devil is disguised as an angel of light, and in the *Mystère d'Adam* he is in such a form as prevents instant recognition. Recognition gradually dawns on Adam because of what this creature *says*, not from his appearance. However, it seems more likely that the poet and dramatist were trying more to equalize blame, rather that to shift it away from Eve completely. Man's joint responsibility with woman for the Fall from Paradise was admitted by Augustine. Though the woman allowed herself to be seduced first, and in turn tempted Adam to disobey God, Adam gave in without resistance, and did not exercise his reason (Augustine of Hippo, *De Gen. ad litt.*, XI, xxxvii–xlii). Anselm (1033–1109) arrived at a similar conclusion. Adam and Eve are both responsible because the name 'Adam' refers to the whole man created on the first day, male and female. The name 'Adam' expresses the union of the two, man and the woman created from his side. If only Eve had sinned, the whole human race need not have been condemned (Anselm, *De Con. Virg.*, ix and x).

Hugh of St Victor insisted also on Adam's consent in the sin. Certainly Eve's relative weakness of reason allowed the devil to succeed more easily with her. At first she might seem more blameworthy, because she herself tempts Adam, but Adam consented without even reprimanding her and so is equally to blame (Hugh of St Victor, *De Sac. Ch. Fid.*, I, vii, 10). Ernaud of

Bonneval also commented along these lines, and indeed treats Adam quite severely. Eve sinned through pride and disobedience, but Adam made no resistance. He compares Adam to Job, and none too favourably. Adam in perfect condition in the garden of Paradise was weak. Job on his dung hill – also subjected to a nagging female tongue – was both strong and humble, able to repulse the temptation to blame his God and also able to reject the words of his wife (Ernaud of Bonneval, *Hex.*, 1548).

Adam in the Bible is inclined to blame Eve rather than himself – he even blames God. When the Lord God questions him, he replies, 'The woman whom thou gavest to be with me, she gave me fruit of the tree, and I ate' (Gen. 3:12). In the *Mystère d'Adam* Adam first recognizes his own sin: *Las peccheor, que ai jo fait?* (Alas sinner, what have I done?), but by the end of this speech he can think of Eve and blame her (356–7): *Ele me dona mal conseil / Ai Eve!* (She gave me bad advice. Oh Eve!) To Eve herself he says (357–8): *Femme desvee / Mal fus tu unques de mei nee!* (Foolish woman. Bad luck that you were born from me!) And before God he blames her in words similar to those of the Book of Genesis:

> La femme que tu me donas,
> Ele fist prime icest trespas;
> Donat le mei e jo manjai
> Or m' est vivre tornez a gwai,
> Mal acointai icest mangier:
> Jo ai mesfait par ma moiller. (417–22)

(The woman you gave to me, she committed the sin first; she gave it to me and I ate it. Now I must live in misfortune. Unfortunately I knew this food. I have done wrong through my wife.)

Eve at first blames the serpent, but very soon is able to take the blame squarely herself, and appears far more honest than Adam.

> Jo sui mesfaite, co fu par (mon) folage
> Por une pome soffri si grant damage
> qu'en paine met [e] mei e mon lignage. (461–3)

12

(I have done wrong, it was through my folly. For an apple I have suffered such great misfortune that I have put myself and my lineage in pain.)

Banished from Paradise, Adam continues to berate Eve in terms which have all the hall-marks of the original anti-feminist outburst:

> Oi! male femme, plaine de traison
> Tant m'as mis tost en (grant) perdicion
> Cum me tolis le sens e la raison! (535–7)

(Oh! Evil woman full of treachery. You have put me quickly in great perdition. How you took sense and reason away from me!)

Adam in the OE *Genesis B* is puzzled by the approach of Satan's devilish messenger, who poses as a messenger from God. The devil's words make Adam suspicious, but so does his appearance:

> . . . þu gelic ne bist
> ænegum his engla   þe ic ær geseah. (539b–40)

(Thou art not like any of his angels which I have seen before.)

He asks the devil for a sign, *tacen*, but the devil gives the sign to Eve. We are told:

> iewde hire tacen   and treowa gehet
>   his holdne hyge. (653–4)

(He showed her a sign and promised faith, his loyal intent.)

The devilish messenger is able to convince Eve that God will be angry with them for not following the command of his 'messenger', because

> hæfde hire wacran hyge
>   metod gemearcod . (590a–91b)

(God had assigned her a weaker mind.)

The devil's messenger was able to deceive the heart of Eve and her weak mind – *wifes wac geþoht* – so that she would persuade her husband. She worked hard at it urging him 'all day' to the deed, until his mind began to waver. Yet Eve, we are told, did it in ignorance and with faithful intent:

> Heo dyde hit þeah þurh holdne hyge, nyste þæt þær
> hearma swa fela,
> fyren earfeþa, fylgean sceolde
> monne cynne. (708–10a)

(She did it nevertheless through a loyal mind, she did not know that so many injuries, terrible sufferings for mankind had to follow. . . .)

Just as Eve's blame is lessened in the poem, their joint responsibility is presented very fully.

> Sorgedon ba twa,
> Adam and Eve, and him oft betuh
> gnornword gengdon; . . . selfe forstodon
> his word onwended. (765b–70a)

(Adam and Eve, the two of them both grieved and often words of sorrow passed between them . . . they thought his word was changed.)

At times they fell to prayer *sinhiwan somed* (both together, 778), and together they uttered many words of sorrow (782). True, Adam cannot refrain from uttering some words of blame to Eve:

> Hwæt, þu Eve, hæfst yfele gemearcod
> uncer sylfra sið (791–92b)

(So Eve, thou hast marked the lot of us both with evil),

and concludes with a wish that he had never set eyes on her (820). Eve, still described by the poet as *idesa scienost wifa wlitegost*, (most beautiful of women, fairest of wives) is as open about her responsibility as she is in *Le Mystère d'Adam*.

> þu meaht hit me witan, wine min Adam,
> wordum þinum; hit þe þeah wyrs ne mæg
> on þinum hyge hreowan þonne hit me æt heortan deð. (824–6)

(You can blame me for it, my friend Adam, with your words; yet you cannot sorrow more grievously in your mind for it than I do in my heart.)

When they go to the wood to find shelter and clothing they pray to God both together, *bu tu|ætsomne* (847), that He should not forget them, but show them henceforth how they ought to live in the light. The interview with God follows after this, with Adam citing Eve's part in the temptation, and Eve the snake's 'fair words' (899) which deceived her, but the idea of joint grief and joint responsibility has already been planted.

It would be misleading to speak of the degraded view of woman created as a result of commentaries on the Fall of Man without considering the most striking rehabilitation of womankind effected by the New Eve, the Virgin Mary. For Ambrose it had been a matter for irony that woman, the origin of evil and lies in the world, had been created within Paradise whilst man had been created outside it. Abelard, in a sermon on the Assumption, noted the creation of woman in Paradise as an indication of her elevation as a sex. Paradise, heavenly and earthly, was woman's natural homeland. Jesus Christ was resurrected on earth, the body of his mother in heaven. From the old Adam was created Eve, but Mary engendered the new Adam (Abelard, Sermo XXVI). Anselm also developed the theme of the New Eve (Anselm, *Cur Deus Homo*, II, viii). As Eve had been a source of sin, Mary was a source of well-being and of blessing. To give hope to women, he pointed to the one woman from whom had come such good, rather than to the one woman who had caused misfortune. Indeed, the Fall of Man could be seen as *fortunate*, since it gave rise to the need for Mary. According to an anonymous fifteenth-century poet, *Adam lay ybounden* for four thousand winters on account of an apple, yet

> Ne hadde the appil take ben, the appil take ben,
> Ne hadde never our Lady a ben hevene qwen [queen].
>
> Blyssid be the tyme that appil take was,
> Therfore we mown [must] syngyn '*Deo gracias!*' (Gray, 2)

St Bernard of Clairvaux, contemporary and adversary of Abelard, also developed the theme of the New Eve in a sermon on the Assumption (Bernard of Clairvaux, *Works*, V, 262–74). Since both sexes had sinned, it was right that both have a place in the scheme of redemption. The new Adam (that is, Christ) takes the place of the old, and Mary takes the place of Eve. In another sermon, on the Nativity of the Blessed Virgin, Bernard saw Mary as reconciling man and woman who had been at odds since the Fall (Bernard of Clairvaux, *Works*, V, 275–88). In this sermon Bernard seems very favourably inclined towards woman. Certainly she is not presented as man's inferior. When Mary, a daughter of Eve, became the Mother of God she showed that Eve was forgiven and that the quarrel between man and woman was ended. Adam, instead of complaining that the woman gave him forbidden fruit, can now claim that the woman has herself nourished a blessed fruit.

In the literature on the Virgin Mary, every sphere of life and nature is searched for symbols to illustrate her manifold virtues, her virginity, her motherhood:

> All that was pure and lovely, all that was high and great, was enlisted in the praise of her glory. She became inaccessible as the walled-in garden, the closed gate or the sealed fountain. She was beautiful as the most splendid objects human art could produce: a decorated shrine, a golden urn, a kingly throne, a palace, a temple and a church. She was mighty and strong as a fortress or as a lofty tower of David. But she was at the same time shy as a young girl, affectionate as a bride, proud as a wife, and venerable as a mother. (Hirn, pp. 325–6)

Her greatness was honoured by reference to the wonders of nature – the earth's fruitfulness, the sea's infinity, the light of the skies. She was to be honoured not just as 'a theological principle or a moral pattern' but

> in her name was worshipped the whole visible and invisible creation as it radiates on us, when it is conceived of as a covering for a spiritual principle, or when it shines in the light of a symbol hidden behind the world of phenomena. (Hirn, p. 326)

Mary's purity was exalted when asceticism was gaining ground in the fourth and fifth centuries. Those who looked upon earthly life and desires as things inevitably polluted took Mary as their guide and ideal, a virgin mother protected throughout life from every physical or spiritual contamination. Traditional commentaries on the Bible accord little goodness or virtue to any women other than Mary herself. Those women whose strength and virtue were such that they could not possibly be held up as examples of weakness and cupidity, tended to be represented as symbolizing the Church itself. Judith, for example, can be seen as representing the Church because she punished enemies of the faith and saved God's people from oppression and destruction. Ruth is the Church of the Gentiles, a foreigner who married a Jew and was faithful to his people. The Church which numbers amongst its members sinners who have reformed can be represented by Mary Magdalene. Even the woman taken in adultery could represent the Church of the Gentiles, which can be unfaithful by worshipping strange gods and yet be saved through the remission of sins by Christ (see Ferrante, p. 26). The Church is also regularly identified with the bride in the Song of Songs. In this instance men are asked to identify with a female role, as the bride represents all mankind, or the whole Church, in its loving relationship with God. But while early commentators concentrated on showing that the bride represented the Church, Bernard of Clairvaux in his twelfth-century commentary on the Song of Songs likens the bride to the human soul, and uses human love to illuminate a spiritual relationship. The human soul is shown as married to Christ because marriage represents the highest form of love known on earth:

> Love is a great thing; but it has degrees and the Bride's is the highest of all . . . it is itself her being and her hope, she is full of it and the Bridegroom is content with it. He requires nothing else from her, for she has nothing else to give. It is this which makes them Bridegroom and Bride; for it is the love peculiar to those

joined in wedlock, and nobody else, not even a child can share it.
(Bernard of Clairvaux, *On the Song of Songs*, trans. p. 259)

Alan of Lille is the commentator who consistently links the
bride of the Song of Songs with the Virgin. This interpretation
forces the reader or listener to move from identifying man's soul
with a woman's role in its relationship with God, to identifying
with one real woman, the most perfect woman who lived and
worked and bore a child.

The development of Mary's stature in the tradition of the
Church put her on the loftiest of pedestals, immaculate from
her conception, virgin before and after the birth of Jesus,
assumed into heaven without experiencing the decay of the
grave. Whilst she was believed to have undone the damage to
mankind wrought by Eve, at the same time she was established
as a model of behaviour which few women could readily
identify with, and as an ideal unattainable by every other
earthly woman. As the most perfect expression of womanhood
she was acknowledged by all men, without changing or impro-
ving the way women in general were regarded. The relegation
of the poor daughters of Eve to an inferior place continued to
find favour in social custom and in the writings of both laymen
and ecclesiastics alike.

2

Holy Virginity

◆━━━━━◆

The connection between woman, the flesh, and matter is at least partly based on woman's ability to conceive and bear children. Isidore, in one of his etymologies, explains that she is called 'mother' because from her something is effected (Isidore of Seville, *Etym.*, IX, v, 6). Mother is the matter, Father is the cause. This inclination towards the flesh was an indication that she was less spiritual than man. Woman's menstruation, indicative of her sex, is also indicative of her uncleanliness. The eighth 'question' addressed by Augustine of Canterbury to Pope Gregory included queries relating both to woman's capacity for bearing children and her menstruation:

> May an expectant mother be baptized? How soon after childbirth may she enter church? How soon after childbirth may a husband have relations with his wife? And may a woman properly enter church at certain periods? And may she receive communion at these times? (Bede, *History of the English Church and People*, I, 27)

Pope Gregory deals with the first question firmly and quickly with refreshing charity:

> Why should not an expectant mother be baptized? – it is no offence in the sight of Almighty God to bear children. . . . On what grounds, then, can God's free gift to man be excluded from the grace of Holy Baptism?

Gregory reminded Augustine of the Old Testament teaching on the space of time which should elapse after childbirth before a woman may enter church – thirty-three days after a male child, sixty-six after a female: 'But this is to be understood as an

19

allegory, for were a woman to enter church and return thanks in the very hour of her delivery, she would do no wrong'. For Gregory, bringing forth children in pain is a penalty for Eve's transgression, but to forbid a newly delivered mother to enter a church would 'make this penalty into a sin', and for Gregory the transmission of this enforced penalty into a sin would be wrong.

Gregory was firmly against the resumption of intercourse before a child was weaned and also against intercourse during menstruation: 'the old Law prescribed death for any man who approached a woman during this time'. But as regards a woman entering church during her monthly courses he showed his straightforward common sense again:

> But a woman should not be forbidden to enter church during these times, for the workings of nature cannot be considered culpable and it is not just that she should be refused admittance since her condition is beyond her control.

He alludes to the woman cured of the issue of blood by touching the hem of Christ's robe, brushing aside the argument that she had a disease, while most women do not, and reminds Augustine that '. . . everything that we suffer in this mortal body through the infirmity of its nature is justly ordained by God since the Fall of man'.

The seeming difficulty in coming to terms with woman's female function in the bearing of children – and her monthly preparation for that function – gave rise to many treatises urging women to keep their virginity and eschew marriage and childbirth and all the troubles that may be encountered in this way. Some of the ideas in the most influential of these treatises will be looked at in this chapter. By comparison with the average daughter of Eve, Mary's purity was exalted by the Church, especially in the fourth and fifth centuries when asceticism was gaining ground. The ascetics regarded earthly life and desires as inevitably polluted, and the Church Fathers set about encouraging virginity as a way of life.

St Paul's plea for continence in I Cor. 7 is undoubtedly one of the main sources of inspiration to the advocates of virginity in later centuries, though interpretations of Paul's words varied greatly. Paul advocated a life of continence, but realized it could not be followed by everyone: 'I wish that all were as I myself am. But each has his own special gift from God, one of one kind and one of another' (1 Cor. 7:7). He said it was better for the unmarried and widows to remain single, but if they cannot control themselves 'it is better to marry than to be aflame with passion' (1 Cor. 7:8). His statements on conjugal rights give equal rights to both husband and wife (1 Cor. 7:3–4), and he does not advocate the exercise of continence within marriage, 'except perhaps by agreement for a season, that you may devote yourselves to prayer'. He says husband and wife must come together again after such a separation 'lest Satan tempt you through lack of self-control' (1 Cor. 7:5). Married people are anxious about worldly matters – a husband is concerned to please his wife, a wife to please her husband, whilst the unmarried can care about the 'affairs of the Lord' (1 Cor. 7:32–4).

This freedom to concern oneself with the affairs of the spirit in the hope of heavenly reward is an argument taken up by later advocates of virginity, especially in women. Tertullian (c.160 – c.225) begins his *De Cultu Feminarum* by urging women to remember the possibility of heavenly reward by eschewing too ostentatious a garb, and 'walking about as Eve mourning and repentant' in order to do penance for the sin they derive from Eve (Tertullian, *De Cult. Fem.*, I, i). He works on the assumption that the fallen Eve would have liked ornaments, thus the woman who wishes to live a new life of grace should avoid them. Such instruments of ostentation as jewels, circlets of gold, dyes for colouring wool, and the black powder for eyelids and eyelashes were, he argues, introduced into the world by the fallen angels (I, ii). Even though he allows that his audience may doubt his sources for such a notion, he goes on to cite how very much less valuable and useful gold and silver are in themselves than iron and brass (I, v). Gold and silver are obtained from mines by harsh and unnatural labour, pearls come from a shell that 'produces some sort of growth inside of it, (and) this should be considered a fault rather than a cause for glory' (I, vi). Even dyeing wool he opposed as God does not permit the birth of purple or sky-blue lambs. These attempts to tamper with nature he believes to be from the devil, and so women should avoid such adornment. In Book I, Ch. ix Tertullian gives reasons for avoiding such adornment: adornment is the result of concupiscence and it causes women to indulge in immoderate living and ambition. In Book II he goes on to explain that modesty is a means of salvation, for a modest woman will dress in such a way as not to make herself the object of men's desire. He goes even further and advocates that women should positively conceal and neglect their natural grace and beauty in order not to cause others to sin (II, ii). However, he does not advocate that women should be slovenly (Ch. v).

Not surprisingly, he is violently opposed to women dyeing their hair. He indicates how unnatural a procedure this is by quoting scripture, but also says it is unpatriotic – for women who make their hair yellow are 'ashamed of their country, sorry that they were not born in Germany or in Gaul'. Thus as far as their hair is concerned, they give up their country. He is also well aware of the damage such dyes can cause to hair. His views on the total covering of hair by virgins as well as matrons he set forth in a separate treatise, *De Virginibus Velandis*. Veiling virgins prevents an upsurge of lust in those beholding them. The worldly young woman courts being seen and learns to dress her hair in all the latest fashions, but the consecrated virgin should wear a veil as the Bride of Christ (Tertullian, *De Virg. Vel.*, ix and xii). The worldly preoccupations to which women fall prey are bodied forth in their love of ornament, and the rejection of such ostentation is right for wives as well as virgins, but the fullest rejection of all worldly splendour is to be found in those who work by 'dedicating themselves to be eunuchs and for the kingdom of God voluntarily foregoing a desire which is so strong and, as we know, permitted to us' (Tertullian, *De Cult. Fem.*, II, ix). Most of his remarks in *De Cultu Feminarum* are addressed to all women but his preference for holy virginity emerges from time to time: 'Dress yourselves in the silk of probity, the fine linen of holiness and the purple of chastity. Decked out in this manner, you will have God Himself as your lover' (II, xiii).

Treatises on virginity from Tertullian to the thirteenth-century English treatise *Hali Meidenhad* exhort their readers to turn away from marriage as a lesser good – if not an outright evil. Of the three grades of chastity marriage was the lowest. The author of *Hali Meidenhad*, puts it:

> Of the three sorts, maidenhood and widowhood and the third wedlockhood, thou mayest know by the degrees of their bliss, which and by how much the one surpasses the others. For wedlock has its fruit thirtyfold in heaven; widowhood sixtyfold, maiden-hood with a hundredfold, overpasses both. Consider then, hereby, whosoever from her maidenhood descendeth into wedlock, by how many degrees she falleth downward. (*H. Meidenhad* 324–9)

Virginity treatises draw attention to the fleshly burden of bearing and rearing children. The author of *Hali Meidenhad* speaks of the miseries of pregnancy: 'Thy ruddy face shall turn lean, and grow green as grass. Thine eyes shall be dusky and underneath grow pale; and by the giddiness of thy brain thy head shall ache sorely' (524–6). With the swelling of the uterus, the pregnant woman's bowels shall have pains, and there shall be 'stitches in thy flank, and pain rife in thy loins, heaviness in every limb'. Her breasts will be heavy with milk, and all her beauty begins to wither, and 'whatever thy stomack disdain-fully receives with want of appetite throws it up again' (527–33). Labour is presented as frightening and painful, when a woman is subjected to the 'indelicate skill' of the midwife. The author of *Hali Meidenhad* does make it clear that he is not denigrating motherhood, merely exhibiting its problems to maidens 'that they be the less inclined to such things' (543). But the encouragement of the holy state of virginity as a means of obtaining salvation does lead to a rejection of the average woman's lot – marriage, possibly more than one marriage, pregnancy, childbirth and family life.

Cyprian's *De Habitu Virginum*, written about 249, was indebted to Tertullian, but was even more influential. He too quotes Paul on the worldly preoccupations of those in the married state, but makes it clear that he himself is not ordering virginity, but is stating a preference. He speaks relatively little about the rewards of virgins, but his views on virgin martyrs are an interesting variation on the grades of perfection in chastity. Martyrdom yields fruit a hundredfold, virginity sixtyfold (Cyprian, *De Hab. Virg.*, xxi). In advocating continence, Cyprian naturally warns against places which would put continence at risk – feasts, even wedding feasts themselves, and public baths are dangerous to virtue. He also advocates avoiding all kinds of ornamentation. His encouragements to virginity include, however, not only freedom to be about the work of God, but freedom from childbirth, and from the dominance of a husband (xxii). In fact in ch. xxii he holds up a life of virginity as an escape from the curse of Eve, alluding to Gen. 3:16: 'You are free from this sentence; you do not fear the sorrows of women and their groans; you have no fear about the birth of children, nor is your husband your master'.

Ambrose addressed his treatise *De Virginibus*, written in 377, to his sister Marcellina. It is possible that he did not know Cyprian or Tertullian's work. His own work uses far more figurative language than theirs. Perhaps this more imaginative approach partly explains its less abrasive and more positive tone. He compares virgins with bees, because they too are hard-working, modest and continent. Holy Church Ambrose compares with a virgin mother, bearing children by the Spirit, not with pain, but rejoicing with the angels. She has no husband, yet she has a bridegroom. Either as the Church among nations or as the individual soul she weds the word of God as her eternal Spouse (Ambrose, *De Virg.*, I, vi, 31).

Ambrose speaks of the flower of virginity, growing in an enclosed garden, quoting from the Song of Songs: 'A garden enclosed is my sister, my spouse, a garden enclosed, a fountain sealed' (Ambrose, *De Virg.*, I, viii, 45). In Book III he, like Tertullian, advises against visiting and against feasts, especially marriage banquets, but his general attitude to marriage as expressed in Book I is quite different to that of Tertullian. In *De Exhortatione Castitatis*, addressed to a friend whose wife had just died, Tertullian's attitude is denunciatory. Starting with Paul's 'It is better to marry than to burn', he says that Paul is not comparing good with good, because one cannot see as 'good' something which is suggested as 'better' than the pain of a punishment (Tertullian, *De Exhort. Cast.*, III). Ambrose insists that he is not writing in order to discourage marriage, but only to speak of the advantages of virginity (Ambrose, *De Virg.*, I, vii, 35). He takes another of Paul's verses: 'He who marries his betrothed does well, and he who refrains from marriage will do better' (1 Cor. 7:28). In comparing marriage to virginity he says that he is 'comparing good things with good things that it may be clear which is the more excellent'. His pre-eminent example of a disciplined life is that of Mary herself, chaste, humble and modest.

By now the virginity treatise could be considered a genre, and both Jerome and Augustine wrote on the subject. Jerome wrote his letter on virginity to Eustochium c.384 (Letter XXII) in the declared knowledge of the writings of Tertullian, Cyprian and Ambrose. At this stage in his thinking Jerome was not severe on marriage, but set himself to exalt virginity. Marriage is a divine ordinance, and virginity cannot be compelled but must be freely offered. He too has recourse to St Paul: 'Concerning virgins, I have no commandment of the Lord' (1 Cor. 7:25). Citing also Matt. 13:8 he concludes that: 'The hundredfold and the sixtyfold harvest come from the same seed of chastity' (Jerome, Letter XXII, xv). He advocates modesty in dress and behaviour, the avoidance of travel and feasting (abstinence from food). When such ideas were disagreed with, as they were

25

in Jovinian's *Commentarioli*, Jerome reacted in a more extreme way by writing his *Epistola Adversus Jovinianum*. Jovinian had advocated that no distinction be made between virgins, widows and the married, and could not approve of abstinence above receiving food with gratitude. He also ventured the opinion that there is only one degree of reward, and one degree of punishment. Jerome's *Adversus Jovinianum* is not only a treatise on virginity, exalting that state above marriage by references to scripture and to secular ideas, giving advice on conduct to virgins and outlining their special rewards, it is also a personal attack on Jovinian. Jerome's virulence has to be seen in the context of his feeling threatened by this attack on his way of life and on a doctrine to which he was particularly dedicated. He considers if one might not think Jovinian fit 'to be bound by a physician's chains when struck by a disease of the mind' (Jerome, *Ad. Jov.*, I, iii). He describes Jovinian's rhetoric as that of a man who 'threw up after vomiting his previous night's drinking' (I, i). On St Paul's 'It is better to marry than to burn', he says:

> For what is merely better calls for comparison with what is worse, and not with the standard of the intrinsically good . . . I suspect the goodness of anything if it is merely the lesser of two evils (I, ix).

His anti-marriage arguments, summarizing what was said to have been written by Theophrastus who died in 287 B.C., are more fully investigated in the section on marriage. The aggressiveness of Jerome's stance probably influenced some later writers on the subject.

Augustine of Hippo also addressed himself to answering Jovinian's approach to the subject in two treatises, *De Bono Coniugali* and *De Sancta Virginitate*. By dividing the subject in this way he made clear the twofold nature of his belief – that marriage is good, a state to be valued in itself and in no way to be denigrated beside virginity, which is sacred. Marriage was 'good' for three reasons: (1) children were procreated by it;

(2) it brought fidelity to the spouses; and (3) it had a sacramental quality. As always, references to St Paul are numerous, even to using quotations in support of marriage which Jerome used *against* marriage. He skirts skilfully around the 'better to marry than to burn' statement by involving his reader in a distinction between sexual intercourse for the sake of procreation and intercourse for the sake of incontinence (Augustine of Hippo, *De Bono Con.*, x and xi). But even intercourse for the sake of satisfying concupiscence is only a venial sin. This is a far cry from Jerome's assertion that paying the marriage debt prevents a man from praying (Jerome, *Ad. Jov.*, I, vii).

Nevertheless, Augustine subtly presents the superiority of virginity in a complex scale of perfection: marriage of the faithful is preferable to the virginity of the unbeliever – a question of faith being preferred to unbelief. He can praise the married chastity of Susannah, the good of the widow Anna, and much more so that of the Virgin Mary (Augustine of Hippo, *De Bono Con.*, viii). In *De Sancta Virginitate* he takes further the arguments touched on in *De Bono Coniugali*. There is less need in his own day for marriage than in the days of the patriarchs. In his day, there is less need to procreate, and more opportunity for spiritual associations (Augustine of Hippo, *De Bono Con.*, ix; cf. *De Sancta Virg.*, ix). He is most careful about the reward of virginity, stressing the foolishness of those who remain virgins in order to escape the worldly cares, the 'troubles in the flesh' of those who are married. St Paul was not discouraging people from an evil (marriage) but from something 'burdensome and troublesome' (Augustine of Hippo, *De Sancta Virg.*, xvi). 'The good of Susanna' is not to be seen as the 'lowering of Mary', nor is Mary's greater good to be considered as the 'condemnation of Susanna' (*De Sancta Virg.*, xix). He gives advice to virgins on their behaviour, but his concern that pride may overtake the woman who has freed herself from the usual vices and blemishes of conduct carries a grim warning, and one for which examples can be found in the history of religious foundations. He knows sure enough that the honour of bearing fruit an hundredfold could well go to a virgin's head (*De Sancta Virg.*, xlvi).

Ambrose had written for his own sister, and it is certain that other virginity treatises like *Hali Meidenhad* or the *Ancrene Riwle* which deals, among other things with chastity, were written with specific women or groups of women in mind. The author of the *Ancrene Riwle* (c.1220) repeatedly addresses his 'leve sustren' (dear sisters). In Anglo-Saxon times a most valued treatise on virginity was written for the Abbess Hildelith and the nuns at Barking. It was written by Aldhelm (born c.640) in the early eighth century. He begins his *De Laudibus Virginitatis* by likening the nuns to bees in the way they industriously collect matter for study. In their peaceful companionship, and in dwelling and working together they are also like bees. Whilst praising their way of life – and thus giving approval to their pursuit of scholarship in history, in the Prophets and the Law, in the Fathers of the Church and in grammar – he also warns them of pitfalls. They must guard against the eight sins (Aldhelm, *De Laud. Virg.*, xi), especially pride. He subsequently wrote a poem on the *Eight Chief Sins* (*De Octo Principalibus Vitiis*), also for nuns' instruction and reading. He recommends reading Cassian, who in the fifth century wrote *Duties of Monastic Life*, the *Moralities* of Gregory the Great, and the Psalms. He has his individual way of referring to the grades of perfection: virginity is of gold, chastity is of silver; marriage is of brass (Aldhelm, *De Laud. Virg.*, xix); also, virginity is wealth, chastity is sufficiency, marriage is poverty. His breadth of learning, so admired by Bede (Bede, V, 18) is shown in the many examples from numerous writers which he brings forward to support his views (Aldhelm, *De Laud. Virg.*, xx–xl). Mary is his shining example, but women saints of Italy and the East also figure. Finally, the preoccupation of virginity treatises with admonishing woman's tendency towards finery is given a contemporary twist as Aldhelm turns to the subject of the personal appearance in the clergy and religious woman. Some of them are partial to coloured clothes, with sleeves striped with silk and trimmed with fur, or some have ribbons and bows sewn on their head-dresses. Some curl their hair with a crisping iron, some pare their nails till they are like the talons of a falcon or a sparrow-hawk. Lest, however, his readers may feel that some of these remarks cut too near the bone, Aldhelm rather charmingly adds that he is addressing no one in particular. The nuns at Barking were apparently well known to him, as in the treatise he addresses Hildelith, Justina, Cuthburg, Osburg, Scholastica, Ealdgith, Burngith, Hidgith, Eulalia and Tecla by name, and at its close he calls his friends 'flowers of the Church, sisters of Monastic life, scholarly pupils, pearls of Christ, jewels of Paradise, and sharers of the eternal homeland'.

This work attained popularity in his own day – there are several eighth-century copies – and was greatly valued through the subsequent centuries of the Middle Ages. Its popularity as a devotional work remained down to the era of printing.

3

Early Monastic Communities

The mention of Aldhelm and a particular group of virgin nuns at a particular time in England prompts a consideration of how such communities began to grow up in England and elsewhere in Europe in the wake of Christianity. Advances in civilization at first seem to have given women fewer and fewer opportunities for independent action, and for exerting their influence upon society. Regulations regarding marriage under Roman Law and then gradually under Church Law gave women a subservient place, overseen first by fathers or guardians and then by husbands. There is some evidence from Tacitus and from early literature that women could achieve prominence amongst the Germanic peoples before the advent of Christianity. However that may be, with the spread of Christianity and Roman civilization in Northern and Western Europe, opportunities for independent women to determine their own existence were few and far between. After the advent of Christianity we have to look more and more to convents and monasteries, rather than to secular life, for signs of prominent female figures.

The exhortations of Cyprian, Jerome and others that virginity confers freedom, not only freedom for spiritual action but freedom from the dominance of a husband, seem to have been accepted wholeheartedly by many women in the so-called 'Dark Ages', and the zeal and energy with which such great numbers of women devoted themselves to the religious life seem to indicate that women valued their independence and achieved it even in an age which is reputed to have demanded nothing but servility from the sex as a whole. To achieve their independence, women had to eschew the normally accepted pattern of domestic life altogether, or give it up at a later stage in their lives after having married and produced their families.

The value of women amongst some descendants of the Germanic peoples took the form of reverence for soothsayers and prophetesses. In Germany proper the early reverence for the Blessed Virgin Mary took over many elements of older forms of worship (Eckenstein, p. 9). The priestly role denied to women by the Church sometimes manifested itself in the more ancient belief in their value as witches or healers, who devised love charms or potions against impotence or the pangs of childbirth (Eckenstein, pp. 6–7). Marina Warner has drawn attention to certain shrines of the Blessed Virgin, such as Montserrat in Spain, which focus on Mary's power to promote fertility in marriage (Warner, pp. 273ff.). Some continental saints are also associated with such activities, for example, St Gertrud of Nivelles, who left a highly-prized cloak as a relic to be hung about women wishing to become mothers. The Anglo-Saxons and Franks were not so eager to connect pagan goddesses or practices with Christian worship, but they seem to have taken very readily to the idea of the monastic life for women. By far the greatest number of women saints amongst the Anglo-Saxons and the Franks are famous because they established and/or ruled a monastic foundation.

Any reference to convent life amongst the Anglo-Saxons, then, has to start by considering the founding of those convents and monasteries. The women who established such houses were usually raised to sainthood and they almost invariably came from one of the ruling families. A noblewoman who received a grant of land from her husband at the time of their marriage could dispose of it as she so desired, together with any land she might inherit from her father. It is this land which was often used to establish a religious house for the lady's own retirement, either during her husband's lifetime or after his death, and as a place for the education and upbringing of her daughters. The freedom of action granted to such women in society as well as the great reverence for the virginal life in Christian thought acted as a spur to the wives and daughters of the nobility to found and enter convents.

Christianity came to the Anglo-Saxons in the sixth century through the ministrations of Irish monks in the north of the country and the followers of St Augustine of Canterbury, sent by Gregory the Great, in the south. From the very earliest time women are known to have played a part in the evangelizing of England. Bertha, daughter of the Merovingian King, Charibert, came to England c.597 as the wife of King Æthelberht of Kent (560–616). As a Christian, she brought a cleric with her who took possession of the older British church of St Martin. St Augustine arrived from France very soon afterwards. At that period the kingdom of Northumbria was gaining in power and importance, ruling territory from the Humber to the Firth of Forth. Probably with a view to extending friendship to such a powerful area, Æthelberg, daughter of Bertha and Æthelberht, was married to King Edwin of Northumbria during the reign of her brother Eadbald in Kent (616–40). Once again, the marriage between a Christian princess and a pagan king was used to extend the faith. One Paulinus was made a bishop by Archbishop Justus in July 625 and sent northwards with her as her chaplain. Bede tells at great length about the conversion of King Edwin (Bede, II, 12 and 13) using the beautiful image of the sparrow swiftly flying through the warm hall in winter time to indicate the brevity of man's life, the mystery of his origins, and his ultimate destination. Paulinus succeeded in converting Edwin, but not before Pope Boniface had written to Queen Æthelberg, urging her to use her influence to help her husband to make up his mind.

My illustrious daughter, persevere in using every effort to soften his heart by teaching him the laws of God. . . . Melt the coldness of his heart by teaching him about the Holy Spirit, so that the warmth of divine faith may enlighten his mind through your constant encouragement . . . . (Bede, II, 11)

Edwin was baptized at York on Easter Sunday 627, with other members of his family. Many Christians now moved to that city, which had once been an important administrative centre under the Romans. The Roman Eboracum became the Anglian centre of Eoforwic. Paulinus was recognized as bishop by Edwin and a church was founded on part of the site of the present minster. Eanflæd, daughter of Edwin and Æthelberg was afterwards a great patron of the Church in Northumbria and especially of Wilfred. With Wilfred she espoused the cause of Rome against the Irish Church in the disagreement about the computation of the date of Easter which culminated in the Synod of Whitby (664). Baptized that same day with Edwin was a fourteen-year-old girl called Hild, Edwin's grand-niece, afterwards abbess of Whitby at the time of the famous Synod.

The first known religious house for women in Anglo-Saxon England was founded about 630 by Eanswith, daughter of Eadbald of Kent, on a piece of land at Folkestone given her by her father. In his *Sanctilogium* (c.1350), which later appeared in an alphabetical arrangement known as the *Nova Legenda Anglie*, John of Tynemouth tells how she resisted marriage to a pagan king of Northumbria by making their union conditional on his being able to persuade his gods to show their power by lengthening a beam. He failed and so departed. A church at Brenzett in Kent is dedicated solely to St Eanswith (Eckenstein, p. 84). When Edwin of Northumbria was slain, six years after his conversion, his Kentish wife Æthelberg came back to Kent with Paulinus and is reputed to have founded a monastery at Liming.

An East Anglian princess, Sexburg, wife of King Earconbert of Kent (640–64), founded a house at Sheppey for her daughter Eormengild. St Mildthrith, who possibly came from Herefordshire, was given land at Thanet as a blood fine for the murder of her two brothers by King Egbert of Kent (664–73), and founded a religious house. A charter of privileges granted by King Wihtred and Queen Werburg to churches and monasteries of Kent at the end of the seventh century names five lady abbesses, including Mildthrith, who place their signatures on the document. The houses named are Upminster in Thanet (St Mildred's), South Minster, a colony of Upminster, Folkestone, Liming and Minster in Sheppey. So at that time Kent alone had five religious houses for women.

Bede (III, 8) indicates that some women went abroad to be educated at this period, just as men did. Two sisters of Sexburg went abroad and became abbesses of Brie in succession. One of Sexburg's daughters also went abroad. St Mildthrith's legend maintains that she was educated abroad at Chelles, and also that she endured being cast into a burning furnace – from which she escaped unscathed – rather than be married (Eckenstein, p. 86).

The most striking representative of this kind of holy woman in Northumbria is Hild, baptized at the age of 14 by Paulinus, though the 'first woman in the province of Northumbria to take vows and be clothed as a nun' according to Bede (IV, 23) was called Heiu. Heiu worked with the blessing of Aidan, who had been brought from Iona by King Oswald, successor to Edwin. Aidan's ministry from Lindisfarne was interrupted for a time by war, and it was after the restoration of peace that he persuaded Hild to take up monastic life in Northumbria. She was kinswoman to the East Anglian king at the time, and had been intending to set out from there for Chelles in order to take up the religious life. Aidan granted her land on the river Wear and she established a monastic way of life there with some companions. But at the death of Heiu she became abbess of Hartlepool in the year 647. Bede speaks in glowing terms of Aidan's regard for her: 'Bishop Aidan and other devout men, who knew her and admired her innate wisdom and love of God, often used to visit and advise her' (Bede, IV, 23). It was from Hartlepool that she undertook the founding of the monastery at Streaneshalch, better known by the name given to it by the Danes – Whitby. It was a double monastery with separate provision for men as well as women. Bede says, 'No one there was rich or poor, for everything was held in common, and none possessed any personal property'. Of Hild herself he says, 'So great was her prudence that not only ordinary folk, but kings and princes used to come and ask her advice in their difficulties'. It was a centre of learning, culture and piety. Justice, devotion, purity, peace and charity were taught to be observed. The inmates were required to study the scriptures thoroughly and apply themselves to good works 'in order that many might be found fitted for Holy Orders and the service of God's altar' (Bede, IV, 23).

A measure of Whitby's success in this field of learning and piety can be seen from the fact that five men who studied there subsequently became bishops. John became bishop of Hexham (687–705), later York, afterwards canonized as St John of Beverley. Ætla became bishop of Dorchester, Bosa was archbishop of York (678–86). Oftfor went to Canterbury to study with Archbishop Theodore and then became bishop of Worcester, and of course Wilfrid became archbishop of York. It would seem that the education and discipline available at Whitby compared favourably with what was available elsewhere, and must have been superior to some. Hild's great power and influence appear to have been wielded with grace and humility, for Bede says that 'all her acquaintances called [her] Mother because of her wonderful devotion and grace'.

It was at Whitby that the great Synod of 664 was held in order to come to a decision about the rival ways – Irish and Roman – of computing the date of Easter. Such was the problem that the king, Oswiu of Northumbria, kept Easter according to the Irish custom, and so had often finished Lent and was celebrating Easter while his wife, Queen Eanflæd, who held to the Roman practice of her Kentish chaplain, was still on Palm Sunday. Differences which had been tolerated during Aidan's lifetime became more serious after his death. He was succeeded by Finan – a 'hot tempered man whom reproof made more obstinate', according to Bede – who staunchly supported the Roman side on the question. He in turn was succeeded by Colman, and it was Colman who represented the Irish side at

the Synod. Wilfrid, educated at Whitby and now abbot of
Ripon, represented the Roman argument. Royalty was present
in the persons of King Oswiu and his son Ealhfrith. They were
divided, for Ealhfrith had been instructed in the faith by
Wilfrid, and King Oswiu, who opened the Synod and passed
the final judgement, held, as already mentioned, to the Irish
ways. Abbess Hild was present, and, according to Bede, supported the Irish. She does not seem to have taken any part in the
discussion, and of course Wilfrid's arguments for the Roman
way won the day.

When Oswiu died in 670, his wife Eanflæd joined her
daughter Ælflæd, who had become a nun. It seems to have been
quite common for a widow to enter a nunnery to see out her
days, even if, as in some cases, she had to found the establishment first. Wilfrid, who succeeded to the see of York, when
Colman was defeated at the Synod of Whitby, went on taking a
most active and important part in Northumbrian affairs for
forty years after the Synod. He was a strong advocate of the idea
that a queen could choose to leave her husband, even during his
lifetime, in order to retire to a religious house and in so doing
find favour with the Church. He made this point abundantly
clear when he supported Æthelthryth (later known as Ethel-
dred or Audrey) wife of Ecgfrith, king of Northumbria after
Oswiu, when she decided to leave her husband to take the veil.
Bede suggests that she had always disliked marriage (Bede, IV,
10) and had preserved her virginity in her twelve-year relationship with the king. She was an East Anglian princess, and
at the time of her marriage of Ecgfrith, who was fifteen, she was
over thirty. Bede maintains that Wilfred himself had told him
that Ecgfrith had 'promised to give estates and much money to
anyone who could persuade the queen to consummate the
marriage' (Bede, IV, 19). She does not appear to have cared
much for the king, but her admiration for Wilfrid caused her to
give him a large property at Hexham, which she had received
from her husband. When she at last persuaded the king to let
her go, it was Wilfrid who gave her the veil, thus breaking all

marital ties, at Coldingham in Berwick. This house had been
founded and ruled by another royal lady, Æbbe, sister or
half-sister of Oswald and Oswiu. Soon Æthelthryth left Coldingham, and went to Ely, to land given her by a first husband,
with whom she is also reputed to have lived in continence. The
Anglo-Saxon Chronicle says under the year for 673, 'And Æthelthryth began the monastery of Ely'. She lived a life of piety and
frugality far removed from what she would have known as a
queen. She must have taken exhortations such as those of
Tertullian and Cyprian to heart, for when affected by a painful
tumour in her jaw and neck, she is said to have attributed it to
punishment for wearing 'the needless burden of jewellery' in
her youth (Bede, IV, 19). She was succeeded by Sexburg who
had founded Sheppey.

Monasteries founded by noble ladies continued to be ruled
by noble ladies, the rule often passing from mother to daughter.
At Ely, Sexburg was succeeded by her daughter Eormengild,
who was in turn succeeded by her daughter St Werburg. In the
south, Barking in Essex and Wimbourne in Dorset also
attained prominence in culture and learning. Barking was
founded in 666 by Earconwald, bishop of London for his sister
Æthelburg. She was succeeded by Hildelith, honoured now
among the saints, for whom Aldhelm wrote his treatise *De
Laudibus Virginitatis*. A one-time inmate of Barking, Cuthburg,
sister of King Ine of Wessex (688–725), founded Wimbourne.
Aldhelm's work seems to have been a great influence upon her,
for she too is a lady who left her husband (Aldfrith of Northumbria) to become a nun.

Evidently noblewomen of the early period could be resolute
and determined in following their own bent; they could be well
educated even if they had to go abroad for teaching. More often
a good education for such women could be had at home in
religious houses founded by their mothers or themselves or
other female relatives. Early education of this kind led many
such women to enter the monastic life for good, where they lived
lives of great piety while at the same time often wielding

considerable power and influence. However, the relative freedom of convent life sometimes encouraged the nuns to indulge
in even the worst of excesses feared by the writers of virginity
treatises. Bede tells of such misdemeanours, as does Gregory of
Tours. Bede wrote critically of the behaviour of the nuns at
Coldingham even under the rule of Æbbe, and the story is told
that Cuthbert at Lindisfarne forbade women to cross the
threshold of his church because of the behaviour of the nuns of
Coldingham (Eckenstein, p. 103). The convent was visited by
an Irish monk Adamnan, a holy man who spent his time in
fasting, prayer and penance, and while there he had a vision of
the destruction of Coldingham by fire. When asked by Æbbe
about it, he said it was to be in retribution for the wicked
behaviour of the inmates. His night 'visitor' had told him how
he had noted everything:

> Nowhere have I found anyone except yourself concerned with their
> eternal salvation. All of them, men and women alike, are either
> sound asleep, or else awake in order to do evil. Even the cells, which
> were built for prayer and study, are now converted into places for
> eating, drinking, gossip, or other amusements. When they have
> leisure, even the nuns vowed to God abandon the propriety of their
> calling and spend their time wearing fine clothes, which they
> employ to the peril of their souls, either to adorn themselves like
> brides, or to attract attention from strange men. (Bede, IV, 25)

Adamnan assured the distressed abbess that this fiery punishment would not happen in her own day. Some efforts were
made to improve things within the convent, but after Æbbe's
death, the monastery really was destroyed by fire. Bede draws a
severe moral from the narrative: 'I have thought it desirable to
include this in my history to warn the reader of the workings of
God, and how terrible he is in his dealings with the sons of men'.

It is in Gregory of Tours that we find an account of the most
extraordinary and bitter revolt of the nuns at Poitiers, shortly
after the death of Radegund, foundress of the house. Radegund
had led a more chequered life than some, having been captured
as a child with her brother by two Frankish kings, Theuderic of

Metz and Clothacar of Soissons. She was given an education, but at twelve became the fifth of Clothacar's seven recognized wives (Eckenstein, p. 53). Her love for charitable work often made her forgetful of her role as royal wife and when her brother was murdered she left Clothacar and was made a deaconess. Once she had decided to devote herself to religion, she founded a house for women outside Poitiers in 559, the monastery of the Holy Cross. She maintained contact with the world, however, as a result of her connection with Clothacar, who had become sole king of France in 558. His four sons divided the land after his death, and Radegund lived through a period of family rivalry and outright warfare, feuding and assassinations. So much is known of her because of her association with two men: one of them was Venantius Fortunatus, a Latin poet who became bishop of Poiters towards the end of the sixth century; the other was Gregory, elected bishop of Tours in 573.

It is his *Historia Francorum* that tells a great deal about Radegund's nunnery. He mentions how she based her Rule on that of Cæsarius of Arles, which she had studied for herself at Arles (Gregory of Tours, *History of the Franks*, IX, 42). He deals at length with the turbulent events after her death. Agnes, abbess in Radegund's time, died in 589. The convent chose Leubover to succeed her, but a certain Chrodield refused to accept this decision. She maintained that as a daughter of King Charibert (one of the four sons of Clothacar, husband of Radegund) she was more suited to rule than to be ruled by such as Leubover. She was joined by Basina, daughter of Chilperic (another son of Clothacar), whom Radegund had prevented from leaving to get married. She persuaded no less than forty nuns to take an oath to help her remove Leubover and put her in her place. They all left the nunnery to get help. The narrative reveals her as a most resolute and fearsome lady. The bishop of Tours would not help her and could not persuade her to change her mind despite the possibility of excommunication. She next visited her uncle King Guntram of Orleans at Chalons-sur-

Saône. Meanwhile, some of her followers had given up and gone away, others had married. She returned and installed the remainder in the basilica of St Hilary at Poitiers and prepared for a siege. Gregory (IX, 40) reports that they were joined by all sorts of ne'er-do-wells. The bishop of Bordeaux assembled with his suffragans of Angoulême, Perigueux, and Poitiers and called on the women to return to the monastery. They refused. The bishops entered the basilica, renewed their request, and, again being refused, they pronounced excommunication. Chrodield, her women and followers attacked the bishops physically and the ecclesiastics had to retreat in no good order – one terrified deacon plunged his horse straight into the river rather than ride to the ford.

Thus heartened, Chrodield decided to assault the nunnery and capture the abbess, and this she eventually succeeded in doing, despite a false start when her followers took the prioress by mistake. The nunnery itself was ransacked and plundered. The story now takes on the elements of a latter-day hostage-taking, with the bishop of Poitiers declaring he would not celebrate Easter – a mere week away – unless a rescue attempt was made, and Chrodield fiercely informing him that should that rescue be made she would have the abbess killed. King Childebert, son of Sigebert (another of the four sons of Clotha-car), ordered Count Macco to put an end to the business by force, and this was in fact what happened, with Macco's men dragging Chrodield out and severely punishing her followers.

Through this account runs the thread of the petty differences and disagreements of a closed community or group, which can so often assume massive importance in the thoughts of one or two aggrieved and aggressive spirits. Chrodield's pride and boastfulness were such that she alienated her own cousin Basina in the course of the affair, and caused the somewhat wayward Basina to change sides. Basina had been given charge of the captive abbess and smartly took the opportunity to get on good terms with her. She changed from this position when one of her followers was killed by one of the abbess', when all were under attack, but later was reconciled with her yet again.

Gregory's account of the bishop's public investigation into the whole disturbance reveals with great bluntness and economy the extent of Chrodield's bitter and vengeful spirit. Chrodield first of all accused the abbess of having a man in constant attendance upon her, a man in woman's dress. She hit on just such an unfortunate person in the company and pointed him out as the one in question. The poor fellow was obliged to explain that he was impotent, and so dressed as a woman. Moreover, he lived over forty miles from Poitiers and knew the abbess by reputation only. A eunuch servant of the convent was also named in criticizing the abbess but a physician came forward to defend him (Gregory of Tours, X, 15). This so angered Chrodield that further venom came forth. In the convent they had risked starvation and nakedness under Leubover and men had been allowed to use their bath. The abbess, moreover, had 'played games', invited 'worldly persons' to dinner, had organized the betrothal of her niece in the nunnery *and* made a dress for her out of a silk altarcloth (Gregory of Tours, X, 16). She had also had an expensive gold ornament made for her niece's neck.

Leubover was allowed to answer for herself and her answers revealed the malice of the accusations. The nuns had never starved though times were hard, and they had more clothes than were necessary. As for the bath, it had been built in Lent and because of the unpleasant smell of the limestone, the Lady Radegund had given orders for the servants to use it till the smell went. It had been in common use by the servants from Lent until Pentecost. Leubover had introduced no new customs in regard to dinner for orthodox Christians; she did what had been done under Radegund and 'it could not be proved against her that she had ever dined with them' (Gregory of Tours, X, 16). Leubover explained about the dress and the altarcloth. A nun of noble family made her a present of a silk robe she had received from her relatives. The abbess had cut off part of this to do with what she wished, and had in fact made her niece a

41

dress. The rest she had made into an altarcloth. She had used scraps *left over* from the making of the cloth to decorate her niece's tunic. As regards the gold ornament for her niece, Leubover called Count Macco as her witness that twenty gold pieces were given to her by the niece's betrothed from which she purchased the adornments quite openly. The property of the monastery was not involved at all. As to games, she only played backgammon as she had done during Radegund's day. It was not forbidden by the Rule, but if the bishops were to forbid it now she would accept their authority.

It is easy to see how facts had been viciously distorted in an attempt to present the abbess in a bad light and justify Chrodield's bid for power. Chrodield and Basina were asked if they accused the abbess of adultery or murder or sorcery or any capital crime, but they had nothing to say in reply, except to reiterate that she had acted 'contrary to the rule' in the matters already mentioned. When their own misdeeds had been reviewed, Chrodield and Basina were excommunicated, and the abbess went back to the monastery. After excommunication Chrodield and Basina went to the court of King Childebert, but even then Chrodield would not give up, 'adding crime to crime, naming forsooth certain persons to the king who not only lived in adultery with the abbess, but also sent messengers daily to his enemy Fredegund'. The hapless Leubover was once more subjected to examination, this time by the king. She was found innocent. Chrodield and Basina pass from history in Gregory's account (Book X, Ch. 20) when he records that they were pardoned and the sentence of excommunication lifted.

4

Nuns in the Later Middle Ages

———◆———

Few nunneries in England survived the Norse incursions of the eighth and ninth centuries without disruption and discontinuity (Meyer, pp. 34–61). Under King Alfred (871–88) great strides were made in re-establishing the English Church and English monasticism. The nunnery at Winchester was founded on land belonging to Alfred's queen, Ealhswith. The royal family continued to interest itself in the restoration and reform of the English Church after Alfred's death, and in the tenth century the English Church was influenced by the great Benedictine monastic reform.

Women in this period, as in the earlier centuries after the coming of Christianity, exercised considerable influence in the establishment and patronage of monastic institutions. Land and property lawfully acquired by inheritance or gift by noble women was used to express their piety in tangible terms. Widows were especially free to deal with their property, queens and royal widows being particularly generous patrons of religious houses of both men and women. Indeed the queen had a duty to protect nunneries after the promulgation of the *Regularis Concordia* in the 970s. Æthelflæd, niece of King Athelstan (925–39), was a great admirer of Dunstan, monk of Glastonbury, who was a great force in tenth-century monastic reform in England. She devoted herself to works of mercy from her house at Glastonbury, and at the end of her life entrusted Dunstan with her estates. With this property, together with that received from his own parents, Dunstan refounded and reformed five monasteries – Bath, Malmesbury, Westminster, Athelney and Muchelney.

Eadgifu, daughter of Sighelm of Kent, became the wife of King Edward the Elder about 920. She saw her stepson Athelstan become king four years later, and after him her own sons Edmund and Eadred. She wielded considerable influence and power, as is borne out by the number of royal charters she witnessed, twenty between 940 and 945 and thirty between 945 and 956. Her pre-eminent position on witness-lists shows how highly she was regarded. She became Dunstan's greatest patroness, so great a friend that her son Eadred is supposed to have caused her to beg Dunstan to become bishop either of Winchester or Crediton. Nevertheless, Dunstan remained abbot of Glastonbury. Under her grandson, King Edwig (956–9), she suffered the indignity of being banished from court and having her possessions confiscated. Monastic revival also suffered under this king, because he inflicted great hardships on monastic communities by confiscating their lands. With heavy taxation he made life miserable for lay people. Dunstan fled to Flanders and did not return till Edwig's successor, Edgar (959–75), reinstated him and made him bishop of Worcester and of London. He held these sees in plurality until he became archbishop of Canterbury in 960. Edgar restored Eadgifu's possessions, but by now she was an elderly woman, no longer able to wield the influence she had once enjoyed. She still attested royal charters though, most of them grants to religious houses. By virtue of her own great wealth, which enabled her to donate land to religious communities, she is believed to have played a very large part in monastic reform in tenth-century England. Edward the Elder's previous wife Ælflæd also seems to have been interested in monastic reform as she is recorded as giving land at Okeford Fitzpaine, Dorset (given to her by King Edmund) to Glastonbury abbey (Meyer, pp. 46–7).

The wives of King Edmund also interested themselves in the Church: William of Malmesbury records that Edmund's first wife Ælfgyfu helped refound the nunnery at Shaftesbury (William of Malmesbury, *Gesta Pont.*, RS, 52, p. 186). His second wife Æthelflæd is also recorded as granting estates to several reform communities. Some lands she gave to her sister Ælflæd and her husband Byrhtnoth, hero of the fight of the men of Essex against Viking raiders immortalized in the OE poem *The Battle of Maldon*. These lands were to be used by them till their deaths and then were to pass to religious houses. Ælflæd's will of 1002 (Whitelock, 1930, pp. 38–43) shows that this is in fact what happened:

> And I humbly pray you, Sire, for God's sake and for the sake of my lord's soul and for the sake of my sister's soul, that you will protect the holy foundation at Stoke in which my ancestors lie buried, and the property which they gave to it as an immune right of God forever: which property I grant exactly as my ancestors had granted it, that is the estate at Stoke to the holy foundation with everything that belongs to the village there, and the wood at Hatfield which my sister and my ancestors gave.

In all this, however, it must be noted that these royal women seem to have been more interested in patronizing piety than in following the life of the pious themselves. Æthelthryth, widow of Edgar (959–75) and mother of Æthelred the Unready, provides an interesting example of a woman who, while acting as regent for her son, used her power of patronage to help secure and consolidate the power of her son's regime. She did so by nominating men and women of her own choice as abbots and abbesses in existing monasteries, and by founding new ones, and in effect treated monastic land as if it was her own personal property. The growth of her power and influence was helped by the provision of the *Regularis Concordia*, the code of monastic observance in England, which made her the special patroness of nuns and nunneries in England. This text, drawn up and approved by the Synod of Winchester (c.970), was translated from Latin into Old English for a community of nuns by Æthelwold, bishop of Winchester. Æthelthryth founded nunneries at Amesbury in Wiltshire and at Wherwell in Hampshire in the 980s and by doing so her support for the monastic reform movement is apparently indicated. Medieval historians and

45

chroniclers have suggested that she founded these monasteries in expiation for her role in the death of her first husband (Æthelwold, eldest son of Athelstan 'Half-king', the powerful ealdorman of East Anglia) and step-son Edward 'the Martyr' (975–8) (Meyer, p. 60). Certainly, the interest of this influential woman in religious foundations seems to have had a strong political bias. In this respect she is unlike the women who were most often associated with monasteries and nunneries in earlier Anglo-Saxon times, whose power and influence arose from their reputation for sanctity.

Royal women did continue to enter the religious life in late Anglo-Saxon times, including during the troubled period prior to the Norman invasion. Æthelgeofu, daughter of King Alfred (871–99), was abbess of Shaftesbury. Eadburh, daughter of Edward the Elder (899–924), was a nun at Winchester, and Eadgyth, daughter of Edgar (959–75), was a nun at Wilton, as was Gunhild, daughter of Harold Godwinsson (January–October 1066). An unnamed daughter of Æthelred the Unready (978–1016) was abbess of Wherwell. The tradition was carried on into the Norman period, as William I's daughter Cecilia became abbess of Caen. The women who continued to rule religious houses had considerable power both in England and on the continent, especially if they belonged to a royal house. Often the abbess would have no other superior, spiritual or temporal, but the king himself. In England many abbesses had the power of a baroness, but, as far as is known, the abbess of Quedlinburg in Saxony, who, under Otto I, actually struck coins, was unusual. Women of this rank were not plentiful, as new foundations after the Norman Conquest tended to be priories not abbeys, and a prioress was of lower rank than an abbess. An abbess/baroness held her land by right of tenure and had the privilege of being summoned to parliament. She had to be a good business woman, able to manage an estate and income, and able to find knights for the king's service, as well as holding her own courts for pleas of debts, the perquisites of which belonged to her.

The new religious orders which sprang up in the monastic reform movement of the eleventh and twelfth centuries took relatively little account of women, at least to start with, and those of Chartreuse and Grandmont none at all. It was Benedictine monasticism which gave rise to the great foundations of Cluny, Cîteaux, Chartreuse and Grandmont. The religious orders of canons were also founded at this time, Premonstratensians and Austin Canons, white and black canons respectively. The Cluniacs devoted themselves to literary and artistic pursuits, while the Cistercians preferred cultivating the land and every kind of outdoor pursuit, interesting themselves in bees, in orchards, in vineyards, in rearing cattle and breeding sheep. For this reason, the Cistercians did not feel they had room for the more delicate sex. Cardinal Jacques de Vitry (1144) in his *Historia Occidentalis* (Vitry, 1597, XV) wrote that the weaker sex could not aspire to conform to such severe rules – nor, indeed, to rise to such a pitch of excellence. Eventually, though, Cistercian nunneries were founded both in France and elsewhere. The position in regard to Cistercian nunneries in England is uncertain. Only two, Marham in Norfolk and Tarrant in Dorset, are mentioned in the thirteenth-century statutes of the Order. Other houses not incorporated in the statutes nevertheless claimed to be Cistercian, and may, as Thompson says have 'followed some of the Cistercian customs in a variety of ways and with a variety of modifications' (Thompson, SCH, Subsidia I, p. 251). Power lists only two Cluniac houses in England between 1270 and 1536 (Power, 1964, p. 1). The richest and most powerful nunneries in England, with the exception of Syon, founded in the fifteenth century, continued to be the early foundations like those of Wessex, Shaftesbury, Romsey and Barking.

Up to this time the pursuit of the religious life had been largely confined to the daughters of the wealthy and powerful, but the twelfth century saw the arrival of two or three – possibly exceptional – men who took an active interest in the religious vocations of people – men and women – of a lower social order.

Such interested men were Robert of Arbrissel (c.1060–1117), Norbert of Xanten (c.1080–1134) in France, and Gilbert of Sempringham (c.1083–1189) in England. Robert of Arbrissel's foundation at Fontevrault appears to have developed from the revival in popularity of the eremitical life at the end of the eleventh century. At first, Robert lived an exceedingly austere and isolated life in the forest of Craon, but when he began to preach, he attracted many people to him. He gathered large numbers, especially women, to hear him, and these women included prostitutes and others of ill-repute. To have such a mixed group of men and women living together in a very unstable and unformed community rendered Robert open to criticism from the Church authorities, and that criticism duly came forth from Marbod bishop of Rennes (PL CLXXII, 1480–6) and Geoffrey of Vendôme (PL CLVII, 181–4). Robert had to accept the need for a formal institution. He began to build dwellings at Fontevrault, to separate the men from the women, and so his foundation began. Robert gradually withdrew himself from the business of running the house after he found a suitable woman to govern it. He attained a certain reputation as a *procurator mulierum*, a protector of women's interests, but this may not be justified (see Smith, in SCH, Subsidia I, pp. 175–84). Certainly his preaching and life-style attracted women (and men) of very different backgrounds and catered for their needs. However, when a regular institution was founded, women of the aristocracy began to take an interest, and widows, spinsters and daughters of wealthy families came to retreat from the pressures of the world. This added to the complexity of the foundation, as well as lending to it a more traditional and 'respectable' air. One of its less respectable noble inmates was Isabella of Angoulême, widow of King John of England, who fled to Fontevrault mainly to escape the effects of her own mischief-making. Her second husband, Hugh 'le brun' of Lusignan, Count of La Marche, was inspired by her to quarrel with Louis IX of France and his brother Alfonso, count of Poitou. She is even said to have plotted to poison Louis and Alfonso. Henry III of England, her son by John, also allowed himself to be involved in her unsuccessful intrigues in France. She lived with the nuns of Fontevrault till her death in 1246 and was buried there.

Gilbert of Sempringham was the son of a wealthy Norman baron and an Englishwoman of low rank. As his lack of courtly bearing and ungainly movement made him unfitted for knightly service, his father gave him two livings, one of which was at Sempringham in Lincolnshire. He had been educated in France and began his teaching career with children, but he attracted many adult followers, especially among the lower classes. His first house was established at Sempringham for women and lay sisters. Later canons and lay brethren were added. The men were canons and followed the Rule of St Augustine, the women followed the Rule of St Benedict. He attracted both literate and illiterate women, clerics and lay-men, and cared for the poor, the sick, lepers and orphans. Girls were admitted at the age of twelve, but could not become novices till the age of twenty. About 1146 Gilbert went to Cîteaux and met Bernard and Bernard's other visitors, Malachy of Armagh and Pope Eugenius III. Cîteaux would not take responsibility for Gilbert's new order, which had spread to other settlements, especially in Yorkshire and Lincolnshire. Gilbert was dispatched home with an abbot's staff, and he lived to a great age, maintaining his contact with the Cistercians through Ailred, abbot first of Revesby and then of Rievaulx. One of the stumbling blocks to a closer tie with the Cistercians was, apparently, the large numbers of women in Gilbert's following. In his order, as in that of Robert of Arbrissel, women were received regardless of their antecedents, wealth or status, and it was this very involvement with lower-class women, some of them prostitutes or criminals, and their living in mixed communities that led to criticism.

However, the medieval attitude towards prostitutes was not, on the whole, hostile, and in general they were encouraged to repent and lead good lives in religious houses founded specifically for the purpose. The great example of the converted sinner, cited from scripture in the Middle Ages, was Mary Magdalene, and the most charitable way of regarding fallen women was as women who had been misguided and exploited, to be pitied, not condemned (See Bullough, 1977, p. 12). Stories of prostitutes who became saints became widely known, such as that of St Mary the Harlot or St Afra. The story of Thais, a Christian who became a prositiute and was later reconverted, was also told in the Middle Ages (See Warner, pp. 127 and 232). Hrotswitha (932–1002), a nun of Gandersheim in Saxony, wrote a drama about the salvation of Thais. Efforts to reclaim prostitutes seem to have redoubled in the late twelfth century, when the houses of Fontevrault and of the Gilbertines were already well established. Innocent III expressed his wish that they should be helped and saved (1198), and in 1227 Gregory IX approved the Order of St Mary Magdalene which set up many houses for reformed prostitutes. In one city at least, Vienna, in the fourteenth century, such a house was organized like a convent, but the women were not bound by vows of poverty or chastity. They could leave and marry if they wished, and many did contract respectable alliances after their period of reform. Though Canon Law warily required public penance and the application for a dispensation before a prostitute could marry (Gratian, *Decretum*, cols 1115–16 and 1155–6), marriage to a prostitute as a means of securing her reform was regarded as a work of charity. The establishment of houses, especially for the care and rehabilitation of prostitutes, is another of the ways in which religious orders developed as a response to the needs of women in the later Middle Ages.

In spite of such developments, most English nunneries continued to accept only daughters of the nobility, gentry or upper middle class as nuns, mainly because of the convents' custom of demanding dowries which only the well-off could afford. Girls of the lower classes could only aspire to being lay-sisters (Power, 1964, p. 14). Also, the lower-middle or labouring classes could always find some useful work for their womenfolk, married or single, whereas most trades and occupations were closed to ladies of the upper lasses. The very uselessness of a noble lady for any occupation other than marriage and motherhood made the convent a significant outlet for the unwanted and unmarriageable daughters of upper-class families. The consequences of this situation will be discussed in the next chapter.

5
The Trials of Virginity

———◆———

The inmates of religious houses were not always at peace with each other, happy in their vocation and glad to stay within their convent walls. The old history of the revolt at Poitiers and Bede's account of the nuns at Coldingham should have suggested that passions could run high and temptations prevail even with those vowed to a life of prayer and seclusion. It was accepted in theory that a woman vowed to God could most successfully follow her vocation if shut up in her cloister, eschewing all but the most distant commerce with the world. Cæsarius of Arles, who somewhat predates St Benedict, in his Rule for nuns (followed by Radegund at Poitiers) had advocated strict enclosure for religious women. Various decrees down to the eleventh century continued to hold to this view. The reformed orders of the twelfth century at Prémontré and Fontevrault were very strict in enforcing enclosure on their nuns, as were the Cistercians and Francisans. In 1299 Boniface VIII promulgated the Bull *Periculoso*, in an attempt to make the enclosure of nuns binding as a law upon the whole Church:

> . . . so that no nun tacitly or expressly professed in religion shall henceforth have or be able to have power of going out of those monasteries for whatsoever reason or cause, unless perchance any be found manifestly suffering from a disease so great and of such a nature that she cannot without grave danger or scandal live together with others; and to no dishonest or even honest person shall entry or access be given by them, unless for a reasonable and manifest cause and by a special licence from the person to whom [the granting of such a licence] pertains. (Power, 1922, p. 344)

The next three hundred years give ample evidence that bishops tried very hard indeed to put this Bull into force, and an almost equal amount of evidence could be produced to demonstrate their failure. General and provincial councils and synods down to the Council of Trent and beyond repeated the ordinance, the need for repetition bearing witness to the continued failure in observance.

In England special efforts to keep nuns within their cloisters had begun even before the Bull *Periculoso*. The Cardinal Legate Ottobon, who came to England during the reign of Henry III (1216–72), enacted constitutions which dealt amongst many other things with the need for the strict enclosure of nuns on lines even more severe than those of the Benedictine Rule. No nun could have a meal outside her house except with her superior's permission, and then only with a relative. Nuns were to remain in their cloister, except at certain times when they were allowed into the chapel, chapter, or dormitory. No secular person could enter these places except for a very serious and sufficient reason. A nun could not speak with a man except in public and in the company of another nun. The head of the house was never to leave it, except for some grave necessity, and if she did so, had to have an honest companion. Bishops entrusted with visitation of convents were to make sure that these injunctions were obeyed.

Some bishops took this task very seriously. Archbishop Pecham of Canterbury (1279–92) carried out visitations to the nunneries in his care and made two general decrees on the subject of enclosure. In 1281 he announced the excommunication of all those who seduced or attempted to seduce nuns. He also returned to the theme of the need for nuns to remove their tempting presence from society and remain behind their convent walls. Later the same year he produced a more moderate statement embedded in a set of constitutions, in which he allows for nuns remaining out of their convents for not more than three days 'for the sake of recreation; or more than six days for any necessary reason'. He also allowed more latitude to those who belonged to mendicant orders.

After the Bull *Periculoso*, further efforts at enclosure were made, but with varied success. One register at least, that of Bishop Dalderby of Lincoln (1300–20), reveals that the bishop experienced having a copy of Boniface's statute hurled at his retreating back as he left the nunnery of Markgate. He had been making a visitation in order to explain the statute (Power, 1922, p. 351). Clearly, a bishop could only do his best in this area, and in general had to be content with regulating the occasions on which nuns left their convents, rather than preventing them from leaving at all. As John of Ayton, a canonist, observed:

> But surely there is scarce any mortal man who could do this [enforce claustration]. We must therefore here understand 'so far as lieth in the prelate's power'. For the nuns answer roundly to these statutes or to any others promulgated against their wantonness, saying 'In truth the men who made these laws sat well at their ease, while they laid such burdens upon us by these hard and intolerable restrictions'. (Lyndwood, *Provinciale*, II, pp. 153–5, quoted by Power, 1922, p. 354)

John of Ayton put the women's point of view very well but whether he saw the justice of it is another matter. However that may be, nuns in articulate revolt against the teaching of the Church clearly have ample long-standing historical precedent.

The revolt must in part be explained by the presence in nunneries of large numbers of women without a true vocation. As mentioned at the end of the previous chapter, becoming a nun was regarded by many as a suitable career for unwanted daughters. Girls of good family became nuns because marriage dowries could not be found for them. Wives and daughters of rebels could be shut away for life in convents (like the two daughters of Hugh Despenser) as a handy alternative to murdering them. Illegitimate children and cast-off wives likewise could find their way to nunneries, as could those who were handicapped or deformed. It is not to be supposed that these women whose vocation had been forced on them were very enthusiastic about repressing natural instincts for freedom of movement and general enjoyment of life. Not all who professed to be nuns were fitted to be chaste, poor and obedient. Chaucer's Prioress in the *Canterbury Tales* had her fine clothes and her dogs (Chaucer, *Gen. Prologue*, 146 and 151). Langland's nun had a child in cherry time (Langland, *Piers Plowman*, B, V, 161).

To sin against one of the monastic vows brought down a penance on one's head, but to leave the convent completely and cast off one's habit was apostasy, and for this the penalty was excommunication. There appear to have been few women who could tolerate the burden of such a ban for long. The apostate nun out of her convent was pursued by all the forces of Church and State. No attempt at marriage could be blessed, but rather cursed; her case would be passed from diocese to diocese, and if this failed to bring her to her senses then the king could be petitioned to send forth his sheriffs and sergeants-at-arms to capture her and return her to her nunnery. Such runaway nuns nearly always came back (Power, 1922, pp. 441ff.). It could be as difficult to break one's religious vows as one's marriage vows. It is little wonder that, notwithstanding the limitations of their Rule, many nuns took their opportunities for recreation wherever they might. The fifteenth-century register of Bishop Alnwick of Lincoln reveals the accusations levelled at the cellaress of Gracedieu, Margaret Bellers, who

> . . . goes out to work in autumn alone with Sir Henry [the chaplain], he reaping the harvest and she binding the sheeves, and at evening she comes riding behind him on the same horse. She is over friendly with him and has been since the doings aforesaid. (Power, 1922, p. 382)

Nuns may well have struck up friendships with any available man – the steward of the convent, the bailiff of a manor, or the wandering harp-player – such as the one Agnes Perry ran off with from St Michael's, Stamford, as also recorded by Alnwick's register. Not many lords or noblemen seem to have pursued or been pursued by nuns, and on the whole the most common story concerns the nun and the cleric. The large numbers of vicars, chaplains and chantry priests were the most likely men to have access to convents and their inmates. In the fourteenth century Bishop Bokyngham of Lincoln threatened nuns with excommunication unless they

> abstain from any dishonest and suspicious conversation with secular or religious men and especially the access and frequent confabulations and colloquies of the canons of the priory of Caldwell or of mendicant friars in the monastery or about the public highways and fields adjoining. (Power, 1922, p. 386)

A visitation of the convent of Cannington in Somerset in the fourteenth century revealed the reality with which such injunctions were attempting to deal. Maud Pelham and Alice Northlode were found to be holding confabulations and worse with two chaplains, Richard Sompnour and Hugh Willynge, in the nave of the convent church. In the same convent one Joan Trimelet was found to be pregnant – 'but not indeed by the Holy Ghost' – and the prioress was guilty of simony.

Only in the context already set out – of forced vocations and emphasis on claustration – can this sort of behaviour amongst nuns be seen in perspective. They were like all women, daughters of Eve, and could thus easily respond to the descendants of Adam when so tempted. In their misdemeanours they were pursued by the servants of God and man. The punishment dealt out fell upon nun and lover alike. The laws of King Alfred (ninth century) treated the ravisher of a nun by fining him:

> Gif hwa, nunnan of mynstere ut alæde butan kyninges lefnesse oððe biscepes, geselle huntwelftig scill', healf cyninge, healf biscepe and þære cirican hlaforde, ðe ðone munuc age.

(If anyone take a nun from a nunnery without the permission of the king or bishop, he shall pay 120 shillings, half to the king, and half to the bishop and the lord of the Church, under whose charge the nun is. *Alfred 8*, Attenborough, pp. 68–9)

The woman likewise was punished in her purse: if she outlived the man she received nothing of his property; if she bore a child, it would inherit nothing either (Attenborough, p. 69). In the later Middle Ages punishment was the prerogative of the Church courts. The two accused could try individually to find a number of compurgators who would take an oath of their innocence. Failure to do this was proof of guilt and penance was given, generally a severe one. In 1286 Sir Osbert Giffard was found guilty of having ravished and abducted two sisters of Wilton, one of them a relative, Alice Giffard. He was excommunicated by Archbishop Pecham and the bishop of Salisbury. The situation was all the more awkward because Sir Osbert was related (though the degree of relationship is not ascertainable) to the abbess of Wilton, Juliana Giffard. Juliana had another sister who was abbess of Shaftesbury, one brother who was bishop of Worcester, and another who was archbishop of York. Osbert's relations may well have encouraged his submission, and did not prevent the imposing of a heavy penance: restoration of the sisters and all goods of the monastery which had been withdrawn; public punishment by being beaten with sticks round the church of Salisbury on three holy days, and on three Tuesdays round the market-place at Salisbury, and similarly round the church and market at Wilton and Amesbury. He was also forbidden to wear a lambswool cloak or any of the trappings of a knight except by the king's grace, and enjoined to serve in the Holy Land for three years. There is some evidence that such severe penances could be commuted if the sinner was sufficiently crafty (Power, 1922, pp. 465–6). But for the nun involved there was probably no escape; imprisonment in chains would be imposed on the obstinate girl till she was sufficiently humbled. She could be made to fast more severely than her sisters, dress more harshly, go barefoot, be beaten by the prioress, forbidden to speak to lay folk again, debarred even from exchanging correspondence. In addition, extra penitential prayers could be demanded of her, and she could be excluded from all convent business, and from holding

57

any office, especially that of prioress. In spite of the ferocity of some of these punishments, lapses continued to occur right down to the Dissolution, with reputation for immorality as much a part of the convent scene as fame for sanctity had been in the early days of Christendom in England.

Part Two

Women and Marriage

6

Marriage in the Early Middle Ages

Four centuries before the Anglo-Saxons came to England, the Roman historian Tacitus, writing of their European ancestors the Germani, described their approach to marriage as austere. Whilst Tacitus may have wished to point a moral to the dissolute Roman women of his experience and make them feel uncomfortably wicked by comparison with a barbarian race, what he has to say is, nevertheless, worth noting:

> They are almost unique among barbarians in being satisfied with one wife each . . . adultery in that populous nation is rare in the extreme. They have, in fact, no mercy on a woman who prostitutes her chastity. Neither beauty, youth nor wealth can find the sinner a husband. (Tacitus, *Germania*, chs 18–19)

Tacitus described the formal marriage arrangements of the Germani. The prospective husband provided the woman's family with a dowry. The woman's parents and kinsmen had to approve of the gifts, which were of a strictly utilitarian nature – oxen, horses, reins, a shield, a spear, a sword. She would have given the suitor a present, most likely arms. In this exchange lay the outward manifestation of the nuptials. Tacitus explained the emphasis on gifts relating to household affairs and war as reminding the girl of her duty to serve her husband in the toils of everyday life and in the dangers of battle. She had to serve him in peace and in war (ch. 18).

The Germani had very little taste for peace, and a chief could only maintain an expensive and demanding troop of companions and retainers by fighting sufficiently often to provide them with spoils (Tacitus, *Germania*, ch. 14). It is by no means improbable that in the course of frequent wars and battles women could have become objects of prey; wife-capture, though not mentioned by Tacitus, must have existed. If the Angles and Saxons practised wife-capture, they probably did so mainly in the transitional period of the actual invasion of Britain. By the seventh century it would have died out, though in the course of subsequent wars and raids, it could have occurred again. Capturing a wife could never have been a very attractive proposition, however, as this kind of marriage would not have brought about ties of kinship between one family and another, links which were of such great importance to Anglo-Saxon society both in peace and in war.

The testimony of the law books points more clearly to the former existence of wife purchase. At the dawn of the history of the English nation marriage was a private transaction, and the exchange of the girl for the gifts of the husband was a sort of sale. The girl's father or guardian received the gifts and she did not have any voice in the matter. In ancient times the person of the woman was most likely the object of purchase, but even in the historical period, a woman remained in perpetual subjection. When the guardianship of her father or other male relative ceased, that of the husband began. The first part of the procedure was the *beweddung*, the pledging or betrothal, at which the bridegroom handed over the *weotuma*, the price of the bride. The girl did not even have to be present at this stage; it was essentially an agreement between two men that the girl be transferred from one to the other. The second stage in the transaction was the *gifta* or actual handing over (sometimes called the tradition) of the bride at the nuptials. The bridegroom gave the bride a small voluntary *morgengifu* or morning gift on the morning following the nuptials.

At a very early stage after the invasion of Britain it must have become customary to pay the girl's father a small sum only, called the *arrha* in Latin, among the Germanic peoples *handgeld*, and to pay the *weotuma* to the bride herself. This development reduced the father's role somewhat. His right was limited to

receiving the *handgeld*, and the *beweddung*, though a real contract, was no longer a contract of sale. Though the *weotuma* or
bride-price was given directly to the bride and became her
property, her property was subject to her husband's control
during his life-time, and so *weotuma* was really a provision for
her widowhood. It would have been payable to her only after
her husband's death. A childless woman who wished to leave
her husband could find this provision taken away from her: *Gif
hio bearn ne gebyreþ, fædering magas fioh agan and morgengyfe.*
(If she does not bear a child [her] father's relative shall have her
goods, and the 'morning gift'. *Æthelberht 81*, Attenborough, pp.
6–7.) In the time of Ine of Wessex (688–726), the first West-
Saxon king to issue laws, penalties were in force for bride-
grooms who did not make the necessary gifts. Equally, if the
bridegroom found that he did not have a satisfactory bargain,
he had the right of redress:

> Gif mon wif gebycgge and seo gyft forð ne cume, agife þæt feoh and
> forgielde and gebete þam byrgean swa his borgbryce sie.

(If anyone buys a wife and the marriage does not take place, he [the
bride's guardian] shall return the bridal price and pay [the bride-
groom] as much again, and he shall compensate the trustee of the
marriage according to the amount he is entitled to for infraction of his
surety. *Ine 31*, Attenborough, pp. 46–7.)

Sureties seem to have been an extra precaution in case the
transaction ran into problems.

The laws of King Æthelberht of Kent (560–616), written in
English before St Augustine, apostle of Canterbury, died in 604
or 605, have more to say about women and their place in society
than those of any other Anglo-Saxon king (D. Stenton, p. 7).
Some of those laws deal with the relationship between man and
wife, and they suggest that woman was regarded as a valuable
piece of property. Stenton does, however, warn us that the
bluntness of the language most probably indicates nothing
more than the inexperience of the compilers in the art of written

63

expression. Law number seventy-seven in Æthelberht's code states:

> Gif mon mægþ gebigeð, ceapi geceapod sy, gif hit unfacne is.
> §1. Gif hit þonne facne is, eft þær æt ham gebrenge, and him man his scæt agefe.

(If a man buys a maiden, the bargain shall stand, if there is no dishonesty.
§1. If however there is dishonesty, she shall be taken back to her home, and the money shall be returned to him. *Æthelberht 77*, Attenborough, pp. 14–15.)

In laws eighty-two and eighty-three we find:

> Gif man mægþmon nede genimeþ: ðam agende L scillinga and eft æt þam agende sinne willan ætgebicge.

(If a man forcibly carries off a maiden, [he shall pay] 50 shillings to her owner, and afterwards buy from the owner his consent.)

> Gif hio oþrum mæn in sceat bewyddod sy XX scillinga gebete.

(If she is betrothed, at a price to another man, 20 shillings shall be paid as compensation. *Æthelberht 82 and 83*, Attenborough, pp. 14–15.)

The laws of King Alfred (871–99) some 250 years later state:

> Gif mon hæme mid twelfhyndes monnes wife, hundtwelftig scill. gebete ðam were; syxhyndum men hundteontig scill. gebete; cierliscum men feowertig scill. gebete.

(If anyone lies with the wife of a man whose wergeld is 1200 shillings, he shall pay 120 shillings compensation to the husband; to a husband whose wergeld is 600 shillings, he shall pay 100 shillings compensation; to a commoner he shall pay 40 shillings. *Alfred 10*, Attenborough, pp. 70–1.)

To present-day sensibilities it may appear that women in the Anglo-Saxon period were in effect the objects of commercial transactions. Yet it must be remembered that everyone, male and female, noble and churl, had a *wergild*, or man-price, as mentioned in *Alfred 10*. A man of status suitable to be the companion to a lord, and thus 'noble', was called a *gesiðcund* man in the laws of Ine, and his *wergild* was set at 1200 shillings. If such a man was killed by accident or intent, his kinsmen, if they did not enter into a blood-feud with the kindred of the slayer, could accept monetary compensation commensurate with his status. The kinsmen of a churl worth a wergild of 200 shillings would also be treated accordingly. Women, as is evidenced by Alfred 10, were treated according to the status of their husband, and so setting a price on a woman is not quite so obviously demeaning when seen in this context. However, there still lurks behind the laws the notion of a woman as property, the damage of which had to be compensated for: 'If a free man lies with the wife of another free man he shall pay the husband his *wergild*, and buy a second wife with his own money and bring her to the other man's home' (*Æthelberht 31*, Attenborough, pp. 8–9). In this case the damaged piece of female property had to be replaced by another piece of property.

Making marriage a matter of financial bargaining meant that just as in any other bargain breaking the contract could be accommodated in financial terms. Like any other contract, a marriage could be broken by mutual consent. It could also be broken by one partner alone: *Gif mid bearnum bugan wille, healfne scæt age.* (If [a wife] wishes to depart with her children, she shall have half the goods.) *Gif ceorl agan wile, swa an bearn.* (If the husband wishes to keep [the children], she shall have a share of the goods equal to a child's. *Æthelberht 79 and 80*, Attenborough, pp. 14–15.)

Direct payment to the woman of the bride-price – what the laws of Alfred called 'the worth of her maidhood' – was indeed a liberalization of marriage custom, and in the tenth century a still more liberal contract came into use. The *beweddung* became a formal contract, without even the one-sided fulfilment through payment of the *arrha*. The agreement was accompanied by sureties to pay the *weotuma* to the bride, and by a solemn act which created the obligation. This solemn act, essential to the contract, originally involved giving and taking a straw, but later on other objects like an arrow or a piece of cloth were to be used. An oath or vow was also substituted for this solemn act and especially in the later Middle Ages, the most popular symbol was a weakened form of the oath, the handfasting. The bride-price and the morning-gift merged to become a regular legal provision in case of widowhood (Howard, I, 269).

In all this, the actual desire and feelings of the woman to be married seem to have been of little significance. Parental or kinsman's will and approval were what decided her fate in marriage, and in the first instance at any rate, conversion to Christianity did nothing to improve the situation. Pope Evaristus (99–105) is quoted by Gratian as saying that 'a lawful marriage is not made unless she is given by the parents'. St Ambrose in *De Abraham*, also quoted by Gratian, commented on the marriage of Rebecca. Rebecca's mother and brother 'called Rebekah, and said to her, "Will you go with this man?" She said, "I will go".' (Gen. 24: 58). Ambrose is quick to point out that Rebecca was merely being consulted as to the day of the wedding, not as to her choice of husband. According to St Ambrose, it did not belong to virginal modesty to choose a husband (Ambrose, *De Abraham*, PL XIV, 453–4). St Jerome in a letter to Amandus also gave his opinion about the women's role in the choosing of a partner. He did not recognize any defect in consent, whether achieved by a bullying father or by a forceful abductor:

> I care nothing for what you say about the violence of an abductor, the offering of a mother, the authority of a father, the whole troop of relatives, the tricks of slaves, the parents' loss of property. As long as the husband lives, even if he is an adulterer, even if he is a homosexual, even if he has been an accomplice in every crime and has been abandoned by his wife for these crimes he is accounted her husband and it is not lawful for her to take another husband. (Epist. IV; see Noonan, 1973, pp. 422–3)

Later on he goes on to ask: 'What is it to be taken by force?' For him the marriage holds good, even if it is constrained by force. However, when Gratian, whose twelfth-century *Concordance of Discordant Canons* gave to Canon Law the shape of a legal system, asked the question 'May a daughter be given in marriage against her will?', he gave consideration to Jerome's and other authoritative opinions amongst both Popes and Fathers of the Church and concluded: 'By these authorities it is evident that no woman should be coupled to anyone except by her free will' (Gratian, *Decretum*, cols 1112–14). In the centuries before Gratian the Church was mainly guided by Roman Law in the matter of marriage consent. Roman Law made consent central to marriage without in any way preventing parents from making the actual choice of partner. A son was enjoined to obey his father's wishes as much as was a daughter, although a son could raise objections to his father's choice without specific reason, while a daughter could only protest if the man selected was base or unworthy. Marriages which went forward at the insistence of a parent were valid in the eyes of the Church Fathers. Parental power did not always work to the disadvantage of the female sex. If a girl's father was at all backward about finding her a husband, she could demand that he made better speed in the matter. Even the Code of Justinian, Roman Emperor from 527 to 565, acknowledged that if a girl reached twenty-five without her parents finding her a husband, then she was not to be blamed for committing fornication, or for getting married without their consent (Noonan, 1973, p. 426, quoting Justinian, Novel 115, cap. 3).

Gratian's belief in woman's freedom to choose was already anticipated in the laws of England more than a century earlier. King Canute (1016–35) issued a great code of law for the whole land, and his concern for the oppressed extended even to women:

> And ne nyde man næfre naðor ne wif ne mæden to ðam þe hire sylfre mislicige, ne wið sceatte ne sylle, buton he hwæt agenes ðances gyfan wylle.

(And no woman or maiden shall ever be forced to marry a man whom she dislikes, nor shall she be given for money, except the suitor desires of his own free will to give something.   *II Canute 74*, Robertson, pp. 212–13.)

The mixture of Christian and Germanic culture present in the Anglo-Saxon people is clearly shown in the tension between Church Law and ancient customs of marriage throughout the Anglo-Saxon period. The complete subjection of woman to man, coming from the East with Christianity, was a notion alien to the Germanic traditions of the Anglo-Saxons. Tacitus wrote that the Germani believed that 'there resides in women an element of holiness and prophecy, and so they do not scorn to ask their advice or lightly disregard their replies' (Tacitus, *Germania*, ch. 8). Nothing specially Christian in the attitude to marriage is revealed in the earliest English law-codes – that of Æthelberht of Kent already mentioned, and that of the joint kings of Kent, Hlothere and Eadric, written eighty years after that of Æthelberht, in about 684–5. It was difficult for the Anglo-Saxons to accept marriage as a bond broken only by death, and they had no strong views about the marriage of nearly related kinsfolk. Conditions of life such as slavery or captivity made nonsense of an unbreakable marriage bond, and so in case of necessity the Anglo-Saxons saw no harm in terminating a marriage. Theodore, archbishop of Canterbury (668–90), went to some pains to reconcile Christian and pagan views of matrimony, but with the conversion still just within living memory, he had to make some concessions to native feeling. He forbade incest and the abandonment of wives except for adultery. But he allowed a woman to remarry after one year if her husband was condemned to penal slavery, and after five years if her husband had been carried off into 'hopeless captivity'. He was unable to make any firm ruling about the remarriage of a person whose spouse had been called to the religious life.

The third code of Kentish laws was issued by King Wihtred in 695 – thus making it contemporary with that of Ine of Wessex

– and dealt almost exclusively with ecclesiastical matters. Four of the laws deal with unlawful marriages. Foreigners guilty of such marriages were to 'depart from the land with their possessions and their sins' (*Wihtred 4*, Attenborough, p. 25). Men of the country were to be excommunicated but did not have to forfeit their goods. Though no definition of unlawful union was given, as this presumably is within the Church's province, penalties were established according to a man's social status. A nobleman who entered such a union was fined one hundred shillings, a commoner was fined fifty shillings (*Wihtred 5*, Attenborough, p. 25). A priest consenting to an unlawful union was to be suspended from his duties pending the decision of his bishop. The laws do not seem to have established any special penalty for the woman entering such a marriage. The uncertainty or even laxity to be found in England in regard to marriage regulations is reflected elsewhere amongst the descendants of the Germani. Though Tacitus praised the faithful and monogamous nature of marriage amongst the Germani (Tacitus, *Germania*, ch. 18), he admitted that their royal families practised polygamy. This was borne out four centuries later by Gregory of Tours in his *Historia Francorum*. Polygamy was probably rooted out quite early, and incest according to the Church's definition of blood relationship, including relationship by marriage, was rooted out with some difficulty in the centuries following conversion to Christianity. Incestuous unions were prohibited in the Frankish, Bavarian, Allemannic, Visigothic and Lombard law codes.

But on the question of indissolubility, the divergence between the Church and the Germanic law codes could be very great. All Germanic law codes allowed a man to repudiate his wife on very slender grounds, by requiring only some monetary compensation for the innocent wife and children. A man could also repudiate his wife for adultery or inability to have children. Frankish law did not allow a woman to initiate divorce. Burgundian law provided that a woman who attempted to divorce her husband was to be smothered in mire. Visigothic law permitted a woman to leave her husband on account of homo-sexuality or if forced to fornicate with another. Roman codes issued by the Visigoths and Burgundians permitted a woman to divorce her husband for murder, sorcery or violation of graves with the possibility of marrying again (McNamara and Wemple, 1976, p. 100). Divorce by mutual consent was recog-nized by the Germanic peoples as it had been by the Romans, and for some centuries after Christianity had spread amongst the Germanic peoples the Church was not able to interfere too deeply in such secular practices. For a whole 300 years after St Augustine had declared in favour of the absolute indissolubility of Christian marriage, the Church seemed to hesitate on the matter. It was a secular ruler, Charlemagne, who in his *Admoni-tio Generalis* in 789 cited the ninth synod of Carthage in prohibit-ing the remarriage of any husband or wife who had repudiated their spouse (*Cap. Reg. Franc.*, I, 56). The matter was taken further when the bishops he had assembled at Friuli decreed that even adultery could not dissolve the marriage bond. Separation in such a case was to be permitted but not re-marriage. The pope showed himself more lax than a secular ruler in this matter when at the Roman Synod of 826 Pope Eugenius II allowed the innocent party in a divorce to remarry in cases of adultery (McNamara and Wemple, 1976, p. 103).

Hincmar, archbishop of Rheims (845–82), took great pains to try to reconcile Church and State in the matter of marriage legislation. He came to the conclusion that both laws should uphold the indissolubility of marriage, except in cases of incest, and incest had to be proved in a legal trial. In the stand he adopted towards the many knotty cases that came within his jurisdiction he was supported by Pope Nicholas I (858–67), though the pope's concern was to establish the ideal of the superiority of the papal court in making final decisions. Some of Hincmar's judgements were of great importance. They include that adultery does not dissolve a marriage; that a separation but not remarriage is permissible in certain cases; that an unconsummated union did not constitute a valid marriage; that a daughter who eloped and married without her father's consent should be excommunicated together with the offending man (McNamara and Wemple, 1976, pp. 111–12). However, the Church in the long run was not going to deem parental consent necessary to a valid marriage. An early clash of views on that subject occurred when Hincmar's judgement disagreed with that of Pope John VIII (872–82) in the case of the second marriage of Louis the Stammerer. Hincmar believed that Louis' first marriage was invalid because it had lacked parental consent. The pope refused to acknowledge the necessity of following this secular custom, and would not recognize Louis' 'second' wife. At this point the issue was not so much defining marriage as defining the whole question of ecclesiastical over lay competence and authority in the matter of marriage law, and in the next 200 years the Church was to move fully into the position of claiming sole authority and competence to judge all aspects relating to matrimony.

The Church's control over the actual marriage ceremony was very slow to develop, and did not really become absolutely formal till the Council of Trent (1545–63). Soon after the conversion of the Anglo-Saxons to Christianity it probably became customary for the couple to attend a bride-mass some time after the *gifta* or traditional ceremony mentioned above. The bride-mass could take place on the day after the bridal night, but it could occur a week or several weeks later. Then the couple received the benediction of the priest on their married life, just as they might receive a blessing for any important undertaking. It was a purely religious act and had no legal significance. Several early spousal services have survived, ranging in date from the eighth-century *Pontifical of Egbert*, archbishop of York (732–66) to the *Red Boke of Darbye* (c.1050), and they consist wholly of prayers and benedictions, some of them very beautiful:

Benedicat vos Dominus et custodiat vos Christus, ostendetque Dominus vultum suum ad vos et det vobis pacem, impleatque vos

Christus omni benedictione spiritali in remissionem peccatorum, in vitam æternam in sæcula sæculorum.

(May the Lord bless you and Christ guard you, and may the Lord show his face to you and give you peace, and may Christ fill you with every spiritual blessing for the remission of sins [and] for eternal life for ever and ever.)

Another says:

Benedicat te Deus Pater, sanet te Dei Filius, illuminet te Spiritus Sanctus, corpus tuum custodiat, animam tuam salvet, cor tuum irradiet, sensum tuum dirigat, et ad supernam vitam te perducat.

(May God the Father bless you, may the Son of God heal you, may the Holy Spirit illuminate you, guard your body, save your soul, irradiate your heart, direct your feelings and lead you into the life above. Spousal Services, SSP, LXIII, Appendix I.)

Though no doubt it was the aim and desire of the Church to ensure that matrimony was duly solemnized in order to prevent the evils of contempt and neglect, its success was often limited to providing a special benediction on the newly-weds, rather than providing an essential part of the marriage celebration. In fact, in the spousal services just mentioned there is no reference to a mass at all, and whether a priest was always present at the solemnization of the nuptials is not clear either. Hincmar of Rheims did actually try to use both secular and ecclesiastical courts to enforce a unified doctrine of marriage. In 860 whilst attempting to make judgement in four different marriage cases, he produced a precise definition of marriage:

We learn from the fathers and find it handed down to us by holy apostles and their successors that a marriage is lawful only when the wife's hand was requested from those who appear to have power over her and who are acting as her guardians and when she had been betrothed by her parents and relatives and when she was given a sacerdotal benediction with prayers and oblations from a priest and at the appropriate time established by custom was solemnly received by her husband, guarded and attended by bridal attendants requested from her nearest kin and provided with a dowry. For two or three days they should then set aside a period for prayers, guarding their chastity, so that they may beget good offspring and please the Lord. Then their children will not be spurious but legitimate and elegible to be their heirs. (See McNamara and Wemple, 1976, p. 108)

The correct procedure for disposing of the woman's body is one of the principle concerns here, as it was with the Anglo-Saxons at the dawn of their history. A wife's duty to obey her husband along the lines advocated by St Paul first appears in England in the laws of Ine of Wessex. A woman could be free from being implicated in the crime of her husband because she had to obey him, and so was not a free agent.

> Gif ceorl ceap forstilð and bireð into his ærne, and befehð þærinne mon, þonne bið se his dæl synnig butan þam wife anum, forðon hio sceal hire ealdore hieran: gif hio dear mid aðe gecyðan þæt hio þæs forstolenan ne onbite, nime hire ðriddan sceat.

(If a husband steals a beast and carries it into his house and it is siezed therein, he shall forfeit his share of the chattels, his wife only being exempt since she must obey her lord. If she dare declare with an oath that she has not tasted the stolen meat she shall retain her third share of the chattels. *Ine 57*, Attenborough, pp. 54–7.)

Three hundred or so years after this, Canute's law code was very careful on the same point. The wife is not responsible for her husband's crime of theft, because a wife cannot forbid her husband to bring anything into the home (there is no mention of her having to 'obey' as such).

> Ac ðara cægan heo sceal weardian, þæt is hire heddernes cæg and hyre cyste cæge (and hire tægan); gyf hit under ðyssa ænigum gebroht byð, ðone bið heo scyldig.

(But it is her duty to guard the keys of the following: her storeroom, and her chest and her cupboard. If the goods have been put in any of these she shall be held guilty. *II Canute 76*, Robertson, pp. 212–13.)

Icelandic sagas which purport to be realistic biographies of Icelanders who lived during Iceland's settlement period (870

73

−1050) give several examples of courtship and marriage problems which suggest that the Church's views on such matters did not much preoccupy the Icelandic descendants of the Germani. A woman's consent was not required by law, and there is no indication that the authors of the sagas thought that her consent was even desirable, although marriages made contrary to the girl's stated wishes were disasters, often ending with the death or maiming of the husband, or divorce. Good solid economic and social considerations were the best foundations for a lasting marriage, and love was not an issue. If a man did not propose soon enough after expressing interest in a girl, especially in these family sagas of the settlement period, he was likely to die. A girl's honour was so precious to her family that a blood-feud could result from its being besmirched even by a tardy suitor. Thordis in *Gislasaga* lost three successive suitors in this way, thanks to her brother's consideration for her honour. Her brother also managed to kill off her first husband, and only at that point did Thordis show sufficient independence to side with her second husband against him (see R. Frank, 1973, pp. 473ff.).

Whilst marriage could initiate a conflict, as in the case outlined above, it was also used amongst the Teutonic peoples in an attempt to end a blood-feud between two warring factions or nations. That this was not always successful is shown in *Beowulf*, in the story of Freawaru. Daughter of the Danish king Hrothgar, she was given to Ingeld, prince of the Heathobards, in order to make peace between the Danes and the Heathobards. Of Hrothgar we are told:

> ond þæt ræd talað
> þæt he mid ðy wife wælfæhða dæl,
> sæcca gesette. (2027b–9a)

(He counted it good policy that he should settle many deadly feuds and quarrels through that woman.)

However, the sight of Freawaru's Danish attendants in Ingeld's hall, wearing armour and heirlooms captured from the Heathobards themselves, so inflamed an aged retainer that he incited Ingeld to vengeance for his father's death. Freawaru's Danish courtiers were attacked and so the old feud broke out anew:

> ond him wiflufan
> æfter cearwælmum   colran weorðað. (2065b–6)

(And his [Ingeld's] love for his wife grows cooler with the risings of care.)

Beowulf himself, alluding to the story of Freawaru and Ingeld, advises:

> Of seldan hwær
> æfter leodhryre   lytle hwile
> bongar bugeð   þeah seo bryd duge!

(For the most part seldom at all is it that the murderous spear lies idle even for a little while, after the downfall of a prince, however good the bride may be.)

What the feelings of the bride herself may have been we can only speculate. They were not deemed important enough to mention in this instance. Earlier in *Beowulf*, the distress of another woman caught in the reopening of a feud between her own and her husband's people is allusively told in the so-called Finn-episode. Strife broke out between the Healfdene (Half-Danes) and the Frisian followers of Finn, to the great distress of Hildeburh, Finn's Danish wife, and sister of Hnæf, leader of the Half-Danes. The magnitude of her grief is only hinted at, however:

> |þæt wæs geomuru ides!
> Nalles holinga   Hoces dohtor
> meotodsceaft bemearn,   syþðan morgen com,
> ða heo under swegle   geseon meahte
> morþorbealo maga,   þær heo ær mæste heold
> worolde wynne. (1075b–80a)

(A sad princess was she! Not by any means did the daughter of Hoc mourn without reason over the decree of fate, when morning came –

75

when she could see in the light of day the slaughter of her kinsfolk where she once possessed the highest earthly pleasure.)

Her brother and son are killed, and she commits *hire sylfre sunu* – her own son – to the flames of her brother's funeral pyre: *ides gnornode/geomrode giddum* (1117b–18a] (the unhappy woman mourned, and lamented in dirges). After a brief truce, hostilities break out again, and Finn is killed. When the fighting is done, Hildeburh's story is completed with the information that she was brought back to her own people by the victorious Half-Danes.

The lyric-elegy known as *The Wife's Lament* is the only OE poem which endeavours to evoke the feelings of a woman who appears to have been abandoned by her husband because of the machinations of his kinsmen:

> ongunnon þæt þæs monnes   magas hycgan
> þurh dyrne geþoht, þæt hy todælden unc,
> þæt wit gewidost in woruldrice
> lifdon laþlicost. (11–14a)

(That man's kinsmen began to think, through secret thought, that they might separate us, so that we two lived most widely sundered in the world, and most hatefully.)

Her reaction is simple: *ond mec longade* (and longing came to me). The anguish of her isolation is suggested in the description of the place in which she has been forced to live:

> Heht mec mon wunian on wuda bearwe,
> under actreo in þam eorðscræfe;
> eald is þes eorðsele, eal ic eom oflongad. (27–9)

(The man commanded me to live in the forest grove, under an oaktree in the earthcave. This barrow is ancient, I am entirely seized with longing.)

The gloomy valleys, the lofty hills, the *bitre burgtunas, brerum beweaxne* (harsh strongholds, overgrown with briars) are summarized in one agonized half-line (32a) as *wic wynna leas* (joyless dwellings). She emphasizes her own loneliness at dawn, by comparison with those lovers on earth who live with their loves and share their beds. The length of a summer's day is conceived by the narrator to suggest, not joyful pastimes, but the weary length of daylight hours which she can only fill with grieving,

> forþon ic æfre ne mæg
> þære modceare minre gerestan,
> ne ealles þæs longaþes þe mec on þissum life begeat.
>
> (39b–41)

(because I can never assuage my care of mind, nor all the longing which seized me in this life.)

Such poems seem only to record brief moments of tragic pressure in the marriages of their female subjects, emphasizing separation, loss and hostility. The proper poetic stance of being grieved by experience, yet giving cheer to others by the appropriate expression of that grief in poetic language (see Shippey, pp. 55–6) would appear to show itself particularly well in the treatment of women in much OE poetry, especially in those poems whose backdrop is that of Anglo-Saxon or Germanic society. These women are women of trials and sorrows, especially in their relations with men.

Of course marital separations could take place for reasons far more mundane than inter-family or tribal feuds. Marriages made for economic or political reasons could be easily dissolved. Many marriages must have ended in separation or divorce. Tacitus' idea that Germanic women lived in a chastity that was virtually impregnable, is probably no more than special pleading: 'They take one husband, like the one body or life that they possess' [Tacitus, *Germania*, ch. 19]. Such customary contentment would have fitted very neatly with Christian views on the exclusivity and indissolubility of the marriage tie. However, the reality for the Anglo-Saxons as for other Teutonic peoples was rather different. From the ninth to the eleventh centuries the Anglo-Saxons were still following their own relatively lax rules about divorce. The marital escapades of

Uhtred, *eorl* or 'under-king' of Northumbria, are an indication of the ways in which marriage could be used and abused to further one man's career – they show also how easily divorce could be arranged. Uhtred married Ecgfrida, daughter of Ealdun, bishop of Durham, on condition that he would treat her with honour as long as he lived. He soon set her aside for Sigen, daughter of a rich Northumbrian called Styr, provided that he slew Thurbrand, Styr's enemy. Ecgfrida, thus released, remarried. Later on, when Æthelred II (979–1016) wished to reward Uhtred for military services and secure his loyalty, he offered Uhtred his daughter Ælfgifu. One must presume that Uhtred put away Sigen in order to receive this third wife. He had not managed to keep his promise to kill Thurbrand – later Thurbrand was to kill him. Poor Ecgfrida also suffered being sent away by her second husband, returning to her father in Durham and bringing back at least part of her original dowry in estates. It is possible that Scandinavian practice had led to a weakening of the value of marital ties in the Danelaw area of the north and east of England in the later Anglo-Saxon period.

Many Anglo-Saxon wills reveal that a great number of marriages were satisfactory, however they may have been arranged, and the general well-being of women was protected by law. Many are the laws in the Anglo-Saxon period imposing penalties on those who rape or abduct women, married or single, nuns or widows. It was the king's duty to protect the helpless, the orphaned and the widowed. The laws of King Canute say that any man doing violence to a widow or a maiden shall make amends by the payment of his wergild [*II Canute 52*, Robertson, pp. 202–3]. King Æthelred had mentioned widows particularly:

> And sy ælc wydewe, þe hy sylfe mid rihte gehealde, on Godes griðe and on þæs cynges.
> And sitte ælc XII monað werleas; ceose syþþan þæt heo sylf wille.

(And all widows who lead a respectable life shall enjoy the special protection of God and of the king. And each of them shall remain without a husband for a year after which she may decide as she herself desires. *VI Æthelred 26*, Robertson, pp. 98–9.)

The desire for widows to remain so for a year is also stressed by the laws of Canute:

> Be wydewan, þæt heo sitte XII monðas ceorlæs. And sitte ælc wuduwe werleas twelf monað and ceose heo syðð þæt heo sylf wille.

(Concerning widows, that they remain for a year without a husband. And every widow shall remain twelve months without a husband, and she shall afterwards choose what she herself desires. *II Canute 73*, Robertson, pp. 210–11.)

A woman who remarried within a year of her husband's death, would lose her morning-gift, and all the property which she had from her first husband, and her second husband had to forfeit his *wergild* to the king or to whichever overlord it had been granted, according to the same law. The same law also cautions against widows being consecrated as nuns too hastily. These kinds of provision throw light on Ælfric's praise of the blessed King Edmund of the East Angles, cruelly done to death by the Danes (870), that *he wæs cystig wædlum and widewan swa swa fæder* (he was charitable to orphans and like a father to widows. Ælfric, *Life of St Edmund*, p. 44). A formulary from the reign of Edmund or Æthelstan gives a clear example of an English betrothal ritual as laid down by law in the century before the Norman Conquest:

1) If a man desire to betroth a maiden or a widow, and it so be agreeable to her and her friends, then it is right that the bridegroom, according to the law of God, and according to the customs of the world, first promise and give a *wed* [pledge] to those who are her *foresprecas* [advocates] that he desire her in such wise that he will keep her, according to God's law, as a husband shall his wife, and let his friends guarantee that.
2) After that, it is to be known to whom the *fosterlæn* belongs [some form of the arrha, no longer paid down, but promised to the guardian]; let the bridegroom again give a *wed* for this; and let his friends guarantee it.

3) Then, after that, let the bridegroom declare what he will grant her in case she choose his will, and what he will grant her if she live longer than he.

4) If it be so agreed, then it is right that she be entitled to half of the property, and to all, if they have children in common, except she again choose a husband.

5) Let him confirm all that which he has promised with a *wed*; and let his friends guarantee that.

6) If then they are agreed in everything, then let the kinsmen take it in hand, and betroth their kinswoman to wife, and to a righteous life, to him who desired her, and let him take possession of the *bohr* [surety for fulfilment of the pledges] who has control of the *wed*.

7) But if a man desire to lead her out of the land, into another thane's land, then it will be adviseable for her that her friends have an agreement that no wrong shall be done to her; and if she commit a fault, that they may be nearest in the *bot* [remedy], if she have not whereof she can make *bot*. (Howard, I, 270–1)

The wording of this formulary indicates the care which should be exercised in committing a woman to marriage. It seeks to ensure the proper procedure according to the laws of God as well as according to social custom. It seeks the woman's consent and contentment as well as her financial security, whether she live close to her kinsfolk or 'in another thane's land'. It also endeavours to ensure that she will have some protection in the event of the marriage not being fully successful.

Such care does not seem to have been taken in the case imagined by the poet of *The Wife's Lament*. The woman's husband in that instance had commanded her to live where she had 'few dear ones, few loyal friends' (16–17). She calls herself a *wineleas wræcca* (friendless exile) in the same breath as she tells how her husband's kinsmen plotted to separate them so that 'we two lived most widely sundered in the whole world in a most wretched fashion' (10–14). Without friends, and sundered from her husband, there is no remedy for her but to lament:

'Wa bið þam þe sceal
of langoþe leofes abidan. (52–3)

(Woe be to the one who must suffer longing for a loved one.)

An historical example of proper care being taken of the woman's interests and an indication of the sort of marriage arrangement which might be made in the latest Anglo-Saxon times is preserved in the record of a marriage settlement from the earliest years of the reign of King Canute (1017–35). It states:

> Here is declared in this document the agreement which Godwine made with Brihtric when he wooed his daughter. In the first place he gave her a pound's weight of gold, to induce her to accept his suit, and he granted her the estate at Street with all that belongs to it, and 150 acres at Burmarch and in addition 30 oxen and 20 cows and 10 horses and 10 slaves. (Whitelock, 1930, p. 151)

The agreement was made before King Canute and attested by the archbishop, Lyfing of Canterbury, and Abbot Ælfmær of St Augustine's (Canterbury), together with the monastic communities they ruled over. The sheriff, Æthelwine, and the names of several other men of Kent are included in the deed as witnesses. Eleven men went forward as security for the agreement when the maiden was produced. It was agreed that whichever of them lived the longest should succeed to all the property and land and no doubt should arise about this matter afterwards: 'Every trustworthy man in Kent and Sussex, whether thegn or commoner is cognisant of these terms'. The terms of the settlement were written out three times, one copy was kept in each of the two churches at Canterbury, Christ Church and St Augustine's, and the third was kept by Brihtric himself. This document is interesting in that while it shows the commercial transaction at the heart of the marriage bond, evident from the traditions of the Germani, it also shows the care which was taken by Christian Anglo-Saxons to ensure the woman's financial security and independence and honour, especially in the event of her being made a widow. Certainly, women had a great deal more freedom and protection in matrimonial matters in the Anglo-Saxon period than they were going to enjoy after the Normans invaded England.

7
The Feudal Wife

———◆———

The coming of the Normans brought feudalism to England. To describe the feudal system as one whereby 'everybody had to belong to somebody else and everybody else to the king' (Sellar and Yeatman, p. 25) is so near the truth as far as women were concerned as to be scarcely humorous. The relative freedom which women of Anglo-Saxon times had enjoyed – among the upper classes at any rate – could no longer be hoped for. Feudal society was essentially a military one, a society which had to be always ready for war if not always actually engaged in war. By far the greater part of England came to be held by a ruling minority of barons who possessed large estates and who held those lands in return for undertaking military duties. Even bishops and nearly all the older and greater abbeys held their estates by knight's service. Baronial estates could in turn be parcelled out into knight's 'fees' (enfeoffment) though even in the late eleventh century barons could choose to retain some knights in their household instead of giving them land.

The amount of service due from each of the tenants-in-chief or barons was generally fixed arbitrarily and without any precise relationship to the value of the holding, though from 1200 onwards the value of an estate was taken into account. A baron had to provide a certain number of knights for military service in the feudal army. Often a baron enfeoffed more knights than were required for the performance of military service. A knight's fee was in no way standardized or uniform in size, varying from four to twenty-seven hides. As early as 1100 there is evidence that knightly service could be commuted by money payment. The practice of paying scutage (shield money) in lieu of service is heard of first in reference to ecclesiastical tenants; it was easier for an abbey to pay money rather than having to maintain men at arms in order to fulfil their obligation of military service.

The lord's estate or manor, embracing one or several villages, was the unit of social organization and had other inhabitants besides the knights already mentioned. The peasant was a villein, a member of the village community, and is sometimes described as a serf. He did servile work, but he was not a slave, though many aspects of medieval serfdom were akin to slavery. He might pay small rents in money or in kind, a few pence or a certain number of eggs, but he had to perform labour services. Labour seems to have been the essence of villeinage. The serf was the lord's chattel, to do with as he pleased, though, hearteningly, he could not be killed, maimed, or beaten by his lord. The lord of the manor reserved a portion of the estate for his own use, known as the desmesne, or the home farm, and this was cultivated for him by his dependent tenants in return for their holdings. The villeins worked regularly two or three days a week, with additional work in the busy seasons of the year. A tenant on a manor could be a free man, and such a man would have paid money rent, and would have performed only relatively light occasional and specific tasks.

This description fits the social organization in most of England in the century after the conquest, but some parts of the country, notably Kent and Northumbria, were rather different. Also in the old Danelaw and East Anglia a more conservative and in many respects freer social arrangement pertained (see Poole, ch. II).

Given such a social arrangement, it is easy to see how a girl, especially of the baronial or knightly class, might be regarded as more or less useless. She could not serve an overlord in war, and this had an unhappy effect on feudal society's approach to marriage. In order to be protected, it was necessary for a woman to be attached to someone who could render military service to an overlord, and who could manage a large estate or patrimony. Thus when a girl was deemed old enough, or if her father was dead, she had to marry, generally with little choice in the matter of a husband. A woman was often merely an appendage to a fief, and it was difficult to separate a woman from land.

Marriage in feudal times reflected the importance for that society of the two-generation family unit – mother, father and children – whose house was at the hub of the feudal patrimony, figuratively speaking. Marriage was a social act of profound importance which protected the patrimony in two ways. First, it linked one family or 'line' to another blood line, through the choice of an impeccable virgin who would mate with the eldest son; second, it ensured that one heir only, the eldest son of such a marriage, succeeded to the patrimony, thus keeping it undivided, wealthy and strong. Limiting the possibility of inheritance to the eldest son of a marriage left the other male children unprovided for and unmarried, and the other males resorted to the Church or to military exploits – and to sexual exploits, provided that those exploits did not interfere with the proper procedure of inheritance within the family. (As the period advanced, marriage did become more and more possible for these hitherto unfulfilled young men. See Duby, pp. 102–3.)

That young wives of good lineage were demanded indicates plainly the role a woman was expected to fulfil in feudal society. She was given by one family to another for the mutual benefit of both houses, but principally as the virgin who would soon become the mother of the next heir to her husband's property. The unmarried women, including widows and those too deformed or handicapped to marry, could be lodged in a nunnery, as mentioned in Chapter 5. Nunneries could be established close by a family's ancestral seat (Duby, p. 93). The young unmarried women were carefully guarded as valuable assets, their virginity a precious saleable commodity to be used to the best advantage when their time came to enter the marriage market. No woman, whatever her class, could be married without the consent of the lord of the manor, and the lord could demand a degrading fine called *merchet* from a villein when that villein wished to give his daughter in marriage. In this way a lord could control the marriages of the daughters and widows of his tenantry, as well as those of his own daughters and female relatives. Marriage and wardship were dealt with more or less unscrupulously. The promise of Henry I of England (1100–35) in his coronation charter that he would take no money for the licence to marry, and would not refuse licence to marry unless it were to one of his enemies, came to nothing. Widows and heiresses were freely sold to the highest bidder or to the friends of the king or overlord, even if those friends were of low degree, to the ladies' 'disparagement'. The Magna Carta of 1215 laid stress on the fact that marriage should be 'without disparagement', that is, it should be between *pares*, persons of equal social standing. As the twelfth century advanced the marriages of male as well as female heirs were controlled by the lord. The lord could give a knight whom he wished to please both a woman and land at one and the same time. The hero of one *Chanson de Geste* is offered a wife and her land even before she has become a widow (Gautier, p. 345):

> Un de ces jorz morra uns de mes pers.
> Tote la terre vos en vorrai doner,
> Et la moiller, se prendre la volez.

One of these days one of my lords will die. I wish to give you all the land, and the woman if you want to take her.)

In yet another *Chanson de Geste* the heroine is not given time to mourn the death of her husband before a second match is proposed to her. She is married within a month of her widowhood, on the very day she is introduced to the new suitor (Gautier, p. 346). The late fourteenth-century Middle English romance of *Ywain and Gawain* (heavily derivative from Chrétien de Troyes' *Yvain*) contains a still more blatant hasty marriage. Ywain slays a fierce knight, and on being sheltered in the knight's castle, falls instantly in love with the widow. The hand-maiden Lunet, who is hiding him, realizes his plight and sets to work on her mistress by telling her that she has no one to defend her any more. Without a knight to do a 'doughty deed' her lands will certainly be lost (954–8). In Lunet's second conversation with her mistress, she works by reminding her that the flower of chivalry did not die with her husband (981–2). On provoking the lady, Alundyne, to ask where as good a man as her husband might be found, Lunet becomes even bolder: if two knights were in the field, she asked, equally well armed, and one slew the other, which was the better of the two? Her mistress' admission, 'He that has the battle', paves the way to a meeting with Ywain. At the very next meeting with Lunet, Alundyne longs to see Ywain: *Bring him, if thou may, this night!* (1062–3). On meeting Ywain, she quickly comes to an understanding with him, and after a consultation with her barons, marries him, her husband's slayer (1251–6). Such speed, which seems to us almost indecent, is typically medieval, and reflects the difficulty which any woman of property had to resist marriage and remarriage, in spite of the Church's theoretical strictures about second marriages. Chaucer's Wife of Bath, sometimes regarded as being larger than life, may not really be so. She is a prosperous business woman who had five husbands.

Marriage in a feudal society was, as indeed it had been in earlier times, a social act of great significance. Its importance was such that social custom demanded a public celebration with great ceremony in order to guarantee the legitimacy of the succession to a kingdom or a patrimony. The bride was handed over amongst a gathering of family and friends in return for a dowry or *dos*, in the form of a ring or a few coins. Finally, in some regions, the kneeling of the bride-to-be before her future spouse indicated that she was going into his power. However, though a young woman or a widow might be married without power to choose or reflect, a girl left an orphan or a widow could demand that her overlord provide her with a husband. If she was lucky she might be given two or three knights to choose from, but the chances of marrying a man she really loved were very small.

Apart from the haste with which many marriages were concluded, another disadvantage of feudal marriage was that a union arranged by the lord or the king might cause bloodshed. A father might wish to give his daughter to one man pending the overlord's approval, while the lord himself might decide to bestow her elsewhere, by way of rewarding one of his knights. The two rival 'suitors' might then feel sufficiently aggrieved to make war on each other (Gautier, pp. 347–8). No less strange a situation prevails in Chaucer's *Knight's Tale*, where the two cousins, Palamon and Arcite, are both struck with love for the beautiful Emelye. They fight over her like wild animals, yet she does not even know of their existence (1809–10). Her brother, Duke Theseus, makes her the prize to be awarded to the one who will win her in the lists, each aided by a hundred knights. Emelye's prayer to Diana (2297–330) reveals that she does not want either of them, and would rather that they made peace with each other. But if she must have one of them, she prays that Diana will send her the one 'that moost desireth me'. Theseus 'awards' Emelye to the victorious Palamon when Arcite's funeral is over. The lack of proportion displayed by the two knights in their quarrel over Emelye reflects upon one aspect of the medieval approach to marriage – the perception of woman as an object to be pursued for the benefit of a man. That Palamon and Arcite regard this pursuit as 'love' when Emelye knows neither of them is ironic. Woman as an object of desire disengaged from any sense of family or feudal feeling, or even occasionally from 'love' itself, is still more depressing to contemplate than woman desired as propagator of the blood line. Old January in Chaucer's *Merchant's Tale* attempts to rationalize his belated desire for matrimony by advancing all the accepted banalities on the subject. He is getting old and needs as heir; he is getting old and a wife will take care of him and his whole estate; he is getting old and has led a life of lechery, so he must put his soul in order before meeting his maker. However, when it comes to the actual choosing of a wife, his age is suddenly of no consequence. He feels himself *stark and suffisaunt* to do all that a man must do (1458–9). He must have a young wife, no 'old beef' for him, but 'tender veal'. The food imagery indicates the area in which his desire lies. The image of the mirror which is used to suggest the manner of his choice of wife

> As whoso tooke a mirour polisshed bryght
> And sette it in a commune market-place,
> Thanne sholde he se ful many a figure pace
> By his mirour (1583–5)

indicates the true level on which his choice is made. A mirror sees only external beauty and not internal qualities, and January picks May because she looks beautiful. Of her wealth or family, if any, we hear nothing, except that she is *of smal degre* (1625). Of her qualities we are to learn a little in the course of her adultery with squire Damien. Marriage is seen as a mercantile exchange, a fitting view for a fictional narrator who is a merchant, but the Tale also reflects one aspect of medieval marriage which was particularly unattractive. January 'buys' his wife and marries her with great speed. She brings only her shallow beauty to the marriage, and even that does not remain January's exclusive possession for long.

Another problem, especially amongst the upper classes, was child marriage. The Church refused to recognize the bond of marriage if contracted before the two 'contracting' parties had turned seven. It further forbade the contracting of marriage unless the boy was fifteen and the girl was twelve. However, the Church seldom dared to state that marriages taking place under those ages were invalid. The *Life of St Hugh of Lincoln* tells of a child who, because she was believed to be a great heiress, was married at the age of four to a great nobleman. Two years later he died, and she was immediately married to another. When *he* died, she was exchanged for 300 marks with yet a third noble bridegroom, and she was scarcely eleven years old. The first husband was excommunicated and the priest who had officiated at the marriage 'in the face of the Church' was deprived; yet the bishop in question never said that the marriage was invalid, and the third husband was enjoying his privileges as a spouse twenty years after his marriage (*Hugh of Lincoln*, pp. 173–7). Richard II of England won his first queen, Anne of Bohemia, by outbidding his royal brother of France for her, though by all accounts it turned out very happily indeed. When she died, policy dictated that he marry again, and for policy's sake his choice fell upon the seven-year-old daughter of the French king. They were espoused by proxy in 1395, and in 1396 they were married at Calais. The author of *Piers Plowman* criticizes his society's mercenary attitude to child marriage:

> But few folk now follow this; for they give their children
> For covetise of chattels and cunning chapmen. (C, X, 254–5)

(But few people now follow this [marrying for the right reasons]; for they bestow their children for covetousness of wealth and clever merchants [subverting a divinely ordained class-hierarchy].)

Often there was a long gap between the espousal or promise of marriage and the actual nuptials because of the young age at which the parties were promised.

There was a continued tendency towards incest amongst noble families which also caused problems. The Church remained outspoken against it, prohibiting marriage within the seventh degree of relationship, forbidding marriage between those related by blood or in the spirit. However, as marriage between cousins could be advantageous to a family that wished to consolidate its possessions, the notion of incest did not appear to trouble many, especially beyond the third degree of relationship (Duby, p. 8). 'Of kin nor of kindred account men but little', says Langland in *Piers Plowman* (C, X, 256). A papal dispensation had to be sought to marry a cousin related within the prohibited degrees, or to marry someone related through sponsorship at baptism. Eventually, the fourth Lateran Council of 1215 reduced the prohibited degrees of relationship from seven to four. The problems in conflicting attitudes towards incest continued over a long period. Though marriages within the prohibited degrees did take place with papal consent, equally, a man who became weary of his wife after a few years of marriage, or who wished to ally himself more advantageously elsewhere, could 'discover' that he and she were related within the prohibited degrees, and could then claim that the marriage was null.

Henry I of England came in for criticism from two different churchmen, Anselm, archbishop of Canterbury, and Ivo, bishop of Chartres, because of the marriage agreements he had concluded for two illegitimate daughters. Anselm in one case pointed out that the couple were cousins in the fourth and sixth degrees. Ivo of Chartres took Henry to task for a similar reason. The king should not permit a union which would have to be dissolved because of the canonical impediment of consanguinity (Duby, p. 26). In order to avoid incest the Church seemed from time to time to be prepared to sacrifice its belief in the indissolubility of marriage, and throughout the period, Church theory and regulations were often modified in the face of the everyday practices of wealthy and powerful noblemen and kings. Fierce criticism from some quarters within the Church, notably from Ivo of Chartres, did not deter Philip I of France when he set aside his wife Bertha in 1092 and took Bertrade, wife of the count of Anjou. On the one hand they were excommunicated three times, on the other Pope Urban II was able to criticize the majority of French bishops for being too accommodating, and for allowing the marriage to be publicly celebrated in the face of the Church. For Philip was careful to give this union the character of marriage, with the bride being handed over in the usual way, and her family receiving a dowry (see Duby, pp. 33–4). As already mentioned, the openness of the marriage was important for the legitimacy of the children born of it, and Bertrade soon produced two sons and a daughter to add to the only son Bertha had given Philip in twenty years. Bertha's son eventually did reign as Louis VI, but at one time the succession might have seemed a matter of concern if that son had died. Concern for the future of his line is advanced by Duby (p. 38) as a telling reason why Philip continued to resist the combined efforts of protesting churchmen, and kept Bertrade.

Less than a hundred years later, that most formidable female of the twelfth century, Eleanor of Aquitaine, was separated from her husband Louis VII of France on the grounds of consanguinity, even though that fact had been known at the time of their marriage. However, a council convoked at Beaugency at the king's request declared the marriage null and void, and Eleanor promptly married Henry of Anjou, soon to become Henry II of England. Contemporary and later discussions of these events tend to suggest that consanguinity was but an excuse to bring about a desired repudiation, a divorce which was wrong and should not have taken place (see Duby, pp. 57–62). Several English chroniclers placed the blame for the divorce squarely of Eleanor's shoulders. She was, by all accounts, an attractive woman, though by no means every commentator considered her charms to be of much benefit. Opinions of her behaviour in this matter varied from feminine folly to outright whoredom (see Duby, pp. 57–61). However, more will be said of attitudes towards women in marriage in the next chapter.

The Church's way of legitimizing such carryings-on did not enhance its reputation. Complaints that the Church made and unmade marriages for money were frequent. Langland makes such a protest in *Piers Plowman*:

In þe Consistorie bifore þe Commissarie he [Charity]
                    comeþ noȝt ful ofte
For hir lawe dureþ ouerlonge but if þei lacchen siluer,
And matrimoyne for moneie maken and vnmaken,
And þat Conscience and Crist haþ yknyt faste
Thei vndoon it vndignely, þo doctours of lawe. (B, XV, 239–43)

(In the consistory court before the bishop's officer Charity does not come very often, for their law-suits last over long unless they obtain silver, and they make and unmake marriage for money; and those doctors of law undo unworthily that which Conscience and Christ have knit firmly.)

And again, Langland writes:

> For a Meneuer Mantel he [Greed] made lele matrymoyne
> Departen er deeþ cam and deuors shapte. (B, XX, 138–9)

(For a fur robe Greed made lawful matrimony dissolve before death came, and created divorce.)

The idea which a less than courtly audience might have of the ready availability of dispensation to kings and noble lords is found in the popular late-fourteenth-century romance of *Émaré*. When Émaré's father, an emperor, wishes to marry his beautiful daughter himself, he sends his counsellors to go and get permission from the pope (232–3), and what is more, he gets his dispensation (238–40). It is left to Émaré herself to express revulsion at the idea that she and her father should 'play together in bed' (254). It must have been thought in some quarters that a king could be permitted to do exactly what he liked.

The role of the Church in marriage for a feudal society has already been alluded to, and it must be said that in theory at any rate, the Church's involvement with marriage introduces notions of humanity and justice where they had often been lacking. The actual effect of Church involvement in many cases, however, was confusion and abuse. Up to the eleventh century, weddings tended to be domestic affairs, socially and ritualistically, designed to promote the fertility of the couple concerned. But the Church could and did give blessings on the newly-married couple, some of which have already been quoted (see Chapter 6). For the Church, the primary purpose of marriage was procreation, and this notion would not have disturbed laymen of the period. Marriages involved the planting of a seed in the female womb, in order to ensure the future of a house, and the continuity of a line. There is some evidence that the Church could be involved even in the domestic rite of a marriage before the twelfth century. Hincmar, archbishop of Rheims, was present at the marriage of a daughter of Emperor Charles the Bald to king Edilwulf of East Anglia in 856, and was invited to bless the wedding gifts and also to give the bride the ring (Molin and Mutembé, p. 28). The early-tenth-century *Durham Ritual* contains seven blessings designed to be part of the marriage ceremony in the home. Two blessings concern the couple, the third the bridal chamber, and the next four have the general heading *in thalamo* (in the chamber). The first two of these again concern the couple, the next the ring, and the last the marriage bed. The *Red Book of Darbye* (c.1061) contains eight similar formulae, suggesting that during this period a priest could be present at all stages of the marriage celebrations. In the eleventh and twelfth centuries the involvement of the Church could be sought by the families of the couple, but of course the Church *wanted* to be involved, to pursue its claims to jurisdiction over the rites, and also to make sure that its conditions for a valid marriage were fulfilled. These conditions were quite simple: there should be no impediment of relationship which might subsequently be used to get an annulment, and the consent of the couple, especially of the woman, had to be truly free. Feudal law demanded the consent of a father and a feudal overlord to a marriage; the Church demanded only the consent of the parties to a valid marriage.

The simplicity of the Church in respect of consent created the problem of clandestine marriage. A private, even secret, consent to marry on the part of a couple, without the consent of parent, guardian or feudal lord, provided it was expressed in words of the present tense (*sponsalia per verba de praesenti*) was held to constitute a valid marriage, even if not followed by cohabitation. A Decretal Epistle of Pope Alexander III (1159 –81) in 1160 to the bishop of Norwich sustained a marriage by private consent against one subsequently contracted and consummated. The importance of the tense in which the words of espousal and the marriage proper are spoken is perhaps more readily appreciated in Latin than in English. Latin at least distinguished present from future meaning with a different form of the verb. English never had a special verb form for the future. So one has to tread carefully between the 'I will' which is an answer to the betrothal question, 'Wilt thou have this woman to thy wife?', and all that followed from it, which indicated an intention to wed in the *future,* and the words in the *present tense* which constitute the actual contract – the sacrament – of matrimony:

> I take thee N to my wedded wyfe to have and to hold, at bedde and at borde, for fayrer, for fouler, for better for warse, in sekness and hele tyl dethe us departe and thereto I plyght the my trouthe. (*York Ritual*, pp. 24–40)

Given that marriage, to be valid, did not have to be celebrated publicly with a ceremony, with witnesses, a person might well find himself married without ever quite intending it, by the use of certain words in the present tense. The formulation of Gratian, in the middle of the twelfth century, that there is no marriage 'until man and woman have been one flesh' also emphasized the nature of marriage as a consensual contract (Gratian, *Decretum,* cols 1062–78). All that was needed for a valid marriage was physical union accompanied by the intent to be thenceforward man and wife (Howard, I, 336). But before the end of the twelfth century the distinction between vows in the present or future tense, coming mainly from Peter Lombard, was introduced and eventually accepted by the Western Church (Lombard, *Sententiae,* lib. IV, dist. 27, 28). A valid marriage could be contracted by saying the right words in the present tense, even without physical union. Physical union, if following on espousals in the future tense, was also held to constitute a binding marriage. For some time the two views on valid marriage ran concurrently: promise to marry in the future tense followed by intercourse, or declaration of intention to marry in the present tense without consummation. Pope Alexander III himself moved from the 'consummation' point of view to the belief in the validity of agreement by spoken word alone. The fact that physical union did take place could be legal ground for assuming the existence of a foregoing promise to wed. This was a fearful trap for the unwary, foolish or downright licentious man or woman indeed, for ecclesiastical courts were apt to judge in favour of marriage unless the contrary was clearly understood. A secret marriage was illegal, and disciplines and punishments might be visited on the couple who contracted one, but it was none the less valid. The bishop of Salisbury in about 1219 issued a rule which forbade a man 'to encircle the hands of a young woman with a ring of rush or other material, whether base or precious, in order the more easily to have his will of her, lest while he thinks he is joking, he binds himself with the burden of marriage' (Powicke and Cheney, II, 87).

It was of course desirable to establish freedom of consent and absence of impediment before the actual ceremony, so at the beginning of the twelfth century a development occurred on both sides of the English channel which placed the marriage rite at the church door before a nuptial mass had taken place. It is not clear whether this new development occurred first in England or in northern France, but it spread from there to other areas (Molin and Mutembé, pp. 36–7). It prevailed into the sixteenth century throughout the western Church (Howard, I, 301). Chaucer's Wife of Bath had married five husbands 'at the church door'. The assignment of the dower would have taken place here, as well as the principal act of marriage, the consent of the parties. Marriage at the church door had as one effect the advantage of ensuring that a marriage was not clandestine. Other measures were also deemed necessary. Since the consent of parent or guardian was no longer considered essential by the Church, the clergy began to take over the function of bestowing the bride on her suitor, and this certainly increased the distinction between private and church marriage. The Church also began to make rules such as that of Archbishop Richard of Canterbury who in 1175 ordered that the celebration of marriage should be public. The constitution of Archbishop Walter in 1200 ordained that a marriage could not be contracted without the banns being published three times in church, nor could it be contracted between persons unknown. The same constitution also stated that clandestine marriages, that is, marriages not publicly solemnized in the face of the Church, could not be allowed except by the special authority of the bishop. In 1215 the decree *Cum Inhibitio* of Innocent III made the requirement of the publication of banns a general law of the western Church, as well as confirming earlier prohibitions against clandestine marriage. This does not seem to mean that marriage was from thenceforth 'ecclesiastical'. But the unblessed marriage was made illegal, and thus involved certain penalties, without its validity being touched. In 1329 Archbishop Simon Mepham ordered that *Cum Inhibitio* be made known to all the faithful, and priests who took part in a secret marriage were to be suspended, and the couple involved to be given due punishment. 'Punishment' would have been meted out either by the bishop's consistory court, or the court of the archdeacon, and seems to have varied from diocese to diocese. In Ely the couple was merely required to have a church wedding with no particular injunctions as to haste, whereas in Rochester the punishment was whipping (Sheehan, p. 250, also Kelly, 1973, p. 440). The punishment in any particular case was at the discretion of the judge. In 1342 Archbishop John Stratford imposed a penalty of *ipso facto* excommunication on those who forced priests to solemnize secret marriages. Nevertheless, clandestine marriages continued throughout the Middle Ages. In fact the commonest matrimonial cause in the Church courts in the Middle Ages was the suit brought to enforce a marriage contract. Individuals seeking divorce were far less numerous than those seeking to assert the existence of a secret marriage contract and asking the court to enforce the contract by a declaration of validity. Most dioceses would then require that the marriage be publicly solemnized in the eyes of the Church (Helmholz, p. 25). Obviously, more than one person was caught uttering words in the appropriate tense to a partner who was prepared subsequently to force a public acknowledgement of those words in court. Some marriages were deliberately kept secret for a long period. It was the revelation of the amorous Edward IV's secret marriage to Lady Eleanor Butler, making his children (including the two young princes) by his queen Elizabeth Woodville illegitimate, which brought Richard III to the throne of England in 1483.

Medieval fiction is not without examples of the secret marriage. Chaucer records no Church ceremony for the marriage of Griselda to Walter in the *Clerk's Tale*, but it is scarcely 'clandestine' (see Kelly, 1973, pp. 442–3). Walter consults Griselda's father, seeks Griselda's consent in her father's presence, and then shows her to his people as his wife. He also *hath hire spoused with a ryng*, before bringing her to his palace. There are more elements of feudal than Church marriage here, and Walter asks Griselda only to obey him without question:

> 'I seye this, be ye redy with good herte
> To al my lust, and that I frely may
> As me best thynketh do yow laughe or smerte,
> And nevere ye to grucche it nyght ne day?
> And eek when I sey "ye", ne sey nat "nay",
> Neither by word ne frownyng contenance?' (351–6)

('I say this, are you ready with good heart to do all my pleasure, and are you ready for me freely to make you laugh or suffer, as I think fit and never to grumble about it night or day? And also are you ready when I say "yes" not to say "no" neither by word nor by frowning expression?')

All he promises in return is *oure alliance*, though later the most severe trial he lays upon her is the apparent withdrawal from that alliance. It is only when the Clerk explains his purpose at the end of the Tale, that some of the peculiarities of the marriage become clearer. The Clerk considers Griselda's humility before her husband, not as an example to wives (that would be *inportable*), but as an example of how every mortal should behave in the face of the trials God sends. Certainly, Walter's proposals and disposals seem more God-like than anything that might reasonably be born from a mortal man. Also, since he is a marquis, and she the daughter of the poorest man in the nearest village, the inequality of the match seems most *un*feudal. The

Clerk's explanation of Walter's coming to Griselda makes the most sense; it is but a parable of how

'God somtyme senden kan
His grace into a litel oxes stalle. (206-7)

In the early fourteenth-century romance of *King Horn*, Rymenhild, daughter of the king of Westernesse, allies herself to Horn in secret. She makes all the overtures, overcomes all Horn's objections, gives him a ring, and fends off two suitors agreed by her father, rather than repudiate Horn, whose queen she eventually becomes. A clear example of a private marriage appears to come in the marriage of Dorigen and Arveragus in Chaucer's *Franklin's Tale*. Dorigen took such pity on Arveragus' wooing that

pryvely she fil of his accord
To take hym for hir housbonde and hir lord,
Of swich lordship as men han over hir wyves. (741-3)

(Secretly she agreed with him to take him for her husband and her lord, of such lordship as men have over their wives.)

As the clandestinity of the arrangement fits in very well with the notion of the couple as lovers as well as spouses – a notion the Franklin makes much of – it seems fair to assume that there is no question of Chaucer forgetting to mention a formal Church ceremony. Dorigen promises to be a *humble trewe wyf*; however Arveragus' promise to obey her like a lover (750) and take only the name and not the power of sovereignty to which he was entitled as a husband complicates the marriage and the plot in the *Franklin's Tale* in a way that prevents consideration of it as in any way typical.

Kelly suggested that it was possible to regard the lovers' relationship in Chaucer's *Troilus and Criseyde* as indicating a clandestine marriage (Kelly, 1973, p. 448). Troilus promises Criseyde *trouth and diligence* (1297), whilst Criseyde states:

'Beth to me trewe or ellis were it routhe:
For I am thyn, by God and by my trouthe. (III, 1511-12)

(Be faithful to me or else it were a pity; for I am yours by God and by my sworn word.)

They also exchange rings, though this is modified by the use of the word *pleyinge*. *Pleyinge* could mean 'jesting' or 'making love'. The precise significance of the rings and the words need not mean marriage, yet in the context could be so understood, a nice point for a consistory court had Troilus been able to consult one. Certainly, he is made to take a more serious view of the relationship than is Criseyde.

The Council of Trent (1545–63) eventually made the validity of marriage depend upon its being concluded in the presence of a priest and two witnesses, yet even Trent declined to give an equal sanction to banns, registration, or the benediction, though these were enjoined in its decree. The Church's gradual take-over of all regulations relating to marriage has often been criticized. Yet Gratian's declaration that 'by these authorities (which he has examined fully) it is evident that no woman should be coupled to anyone except by her free will' actually provided an ideal against which to set the feudal demands of the overlord and the age-old power of the parent or guardian (Gratian, *Decretum*, cols 1112–14, also Noonan, 1973, p. 422). Gratian also stated firmly that 'a father's oath cannot compel a girl to marry one to whom she has never assented' (Gratian, *Decretum*, col. 1113, Noonan, 1973, p. 420). And he was also firm on the subject of the nature of the consent involved in marriage. It was not merely a lustful desire for physical union, nor even some kind of intellectual consent to live together and share one's life. For Gratian, consent was based on 'marital affection', a positive assent to the other person as a spouse (Noonan, 1967, pp. 489–99). This was an element which could not be supplied by family, by feudal overlord, or even by the Church. Of course, families continued to try to ignore such niceties of consent. As late as the middle of the fifteenth century the *Paston Letters* reveal the story of Elizabeth Paston, whose mother Agnes was determined to be rid of her to social and monetary advantage. A widower called Stephen Scrope was found for her. He was about fifty, and had an adult daughter. He was also permanently disfigured as a result of illness. Elizabeth said 'no'. Her refusal of the match was certainly her privilege, but her astounded family made her pay for it. She was shut away, allowed to speak to no one, not even a servant. She was beaten once or twice a week *and some tyme twyes on o* [*one*] *day, and hir hed broken in to or thre places* (*The Paston Letters*, letter 446, II, 32). This went on for quite some time. Negotiations with Scrope were broken off, and nearly ten years later Elizabeth did marry, not once but twice. Her two marriages made her one of the wealthiest women in England.

Elizabeth's seventeen-year-old niece Margery fell foul of the family, not by refusing marriage, but by binding herself clandestinely to the family bailiff, Richard Calle (*The Paston Letters*, letter 861, II, 498–500; also letter 203, I, 341–4). The family had been attempting to marry her advantageously since the age of fourteen. After her secret marriage, her family kept her incommunicado for about two years. Three years after the vows were made, in 1469, the matter came to the attention of the bishop of Norwich, who, after endeavouring to persuade Margery to change her mind, proclaimed that the marriage was valid. Margery's penalty was to be socially ostracized. She was barred from home permanently, and seems to have been regarded as dead. Oddly enough, her husband continued in the Paston employ for several years, but the letters addressed to him never once indicate any recognition of family ties (Haskell, 1973, p. 468). The story betrays the unevenness in the judgement meted out to a man and a woman in such a case, as well as the difference between the social and the religious judgement on such a match.

Though the Church desired that neither family nor state should control so sacred a matter as matrimony, the power of the individual to marry whom he or she pleased was placed by Gratian even above the legislation of the Church itself. The Church's own regulations on the publicity of marriage had to yield to the power of individual consent, even if privately given, and the Church's strictures on incest also had to yield to the belief in indissolubility based on consent and marital affection. Equality of both sexes before God was vindicated by such decisions as Gratian's and though there may have been discrepancy between the ideal and the actual social practice, such discrepancy is hardly a feature confined to the Middle Ages. Psychological and social pressure continued to be put on sons as well as daughters to marry as their families desired. Yet marriages annulled because of extreme coercion were not at all common in the 400 years after Gratian (Noonan, 1973, p. 433). Even sensitive, poetic explorations of the nature of love and its relationship to marriage, such as is found in Chaucer's *Parlement of Foulys*, suggest that power to choose one's marriage partner freely should have its limitations. The question of 'disparagement', mentioned earlier, would have been intended to prevent 'unequal' matches of the king and the beggar-maid variety. The world of the *Parlement*, benignly ruled over by Nature, Vice-Regent of God, suggests quite firmly that love can only exist between equals. There has to be voluntary choice within a given range of rank and order, just as an eagle cannot mate with a duck. Every bird in the assembly is commanded by Dame Nature to take *his owne place* (320), in order that the choosing of mates – the principal reason for the St Valentine's day gathering – shall take place in the proper order, beginning with the *tersel egle*, a royal bird:

> And after hym by ordre shul ye chese,
> After youre kynde, everich as yow lyketh,
> And, as youre hap is, shul ye wynne or lese.
> But which of you that love most entriketh,
> God sende hym hire that sorest for hym syketh! (400–5)

(And after him you must choose in hierarchical order, according to your species, each one as it pleases you, and as your luck is, you will win or lose. But those of you whom love affects the most, may God send him the one [female] who sighs most ardently for him!)

Thus speaks Nature, making it clear that choice based on love can only operate within certain appropriate limits. Many marriages were probably the mixture of arrangement and consent outlined by Langland in *Piers Plowman:*

And þus was wedlok ywroȝt with a mene persone
First by þe fadres wille and the frendes conseille
And siþenes by assent of hemself as þei two myȝte acorde;
And þus was wedlok ywroȝt and God hymself it made. (B, IX, 113–16)

(And thus was wedlock made by an intermediary, first by the father's will and the friends' advice, and then by their own consent as the two of them might agree, and thus was wedlock accomplished and God himself made it.)

Some medieval poets present us with examples of women who did their own choosing, and wooing too. The 'forward female' was as old for the fourteenth century as Potiphar's wife, and as recent as the chatelaine in *Sir Gawain and the Green Knight*. There must have been women who made up their own minds about a mate and acted as rapidly as Rymenhild in *King Horn*. She loved her kingly father's foundling so much that she 'grew wild' (252), and when she sends for him, throws her arms about him and kisses him, offering herself as his wife. Horn's careful reply is directed towards the disparity in their situations. It would be 'no fair wedding' between a thral and royalty (423–4). However, Rymenhild, with great presence of mind, does not argue, but faints. By the time Horn has brought her round, with many kisses, he is ready to agree to her advice provided she helps him to a knighthood. Belisaunt in *Amis and Amiloun* is even more enterprising and ruthless. She threatens to tear her clothes and cry rape if Amiloun will not do as she asks (625–36). In these two popular romances there may be some elements of misconception: a king or nobleman's daughter can arrange things to her own satisfaction where a lesser woman cannot. Yet the middle-class Wife of Bath's foresight in 'booking' her fifth husband before the fourth is dead indicates that such a woman knew well how to look after her own inclinations in the marriage market, provided she was given half a chance. Dame Alice's Tale of the knight who is seen first as a rapist and who ends up being married to an old hag, recognizes a longing to be even with men who can cause much misery by so casual an exercise of power over women. That the same old hag can become a beautiful young woman when the knight agrees to giving her the mastery in the relationship, suggests the existence of a desire for an approach to marriage which is different from the strictures of both Church and State.

The ideal of the freedom of individual consent in marriage for both sexes irrespective of wealth or status which emerged in the later Middle Ages was probably familiar only to a minority of people, churchmen and courageous lay people, especially women like Elizabeth Paston and her niece Margery, who suffered to uphold it.

8

Wayward Woman or Perfect Wife

———◆———

Juan de Torquemada (1388–1468), writer of a commentary on Gratian, yoked Paul's teaching in Ephesians (5:20–5), that husbands should love their wives as Christ loved the Church, with Gratian's statement on individual freedom of consent in marriage, when he wrote

> Marriage signifies the union of Christ and the Church which is made through the liberality of love. Therefore it cannot be made by coerced consent.

The generous spirit of such a statement is not always evident in all Churchmen's approach to marriage in the Middle Ages. Indeed, the Church's 'approach' in the writings of the Fathers and later theologians was not always single-minded. Some approaches and attitudes will be looked at in this chapter. Marriage was already reckoned a sacrament by Hincmar of Rheims, and from St Thomas Aquinas onwards the schoolmen taught that it conferred grace. The general teaching that marriage is a sacrament went back to St Paul:

> For this cause shall a man leave his father and mother and be joined to his wife, and the two shall become one flesh. This mystery is a profound one, and I am saying that it refers to Christ and the Church; however, let each one of you love his wife as himself, and let the wife see that she respects her husband. (Eph. 5:31–3)

But even given that marriage was a sacrament and a good and positive vehicle of grace, the Church's attitude towards it was much influenced by a strong ascetic tradition. Asceticism had been taken over by the infant Church from the stoics, and found its first expression in the early Christians' preparation for martyrdom, and in the exaltation of virginity as a complete consecration of soul and body to God. Asceticism grew apace with the influence of the Desert Fathers in the third century and the beginnings of monasticism in the fourth, and it encouraged a quest for perfection in the Christian man.

St Paul, as mentioned in Chapter 2, had written to the Corinthians that 'if they could not exercise self-control, they should marry, for it is better to marry than to be aflame with passion' (1 Cor. 7:8–9). This and other statements from St Paul were used to form the foundation of a line of teaching which held the superiority of virginity over the married state. In fact, St Paul indicates that he is speaking 'by way of concession, not of command' (1 Cor. 7:6). Chaucer's Wife of Bath, herself so enthusiastic about marriage in the wake of her own five ventures into that blessed state, is very quick to remind her audience of this:

> Th'apostel, whan he speketh of maydenhede,
> He seyde that precept therof hadde he noon.
> Men may conseille a womman to been oon,
> But conseillyng is no comandement. (64–7)

(The apostle [Paul], when he speaks of virginity, said that he had no precept concerning it. Men can counsel a woman to be one, but counselling is no commandment.)

Paul realized that everyone could not follow such advice and that every man has his 'special gift', each one different from the next. The Wife of Bath begins to build her case in favour of marriage on this very foundation:

> But this word is nat taken of every wight; . . .
> But nathelees, thogh that he [Paul] wroot and sayde
> He wolde that every wight were swich as he,
> Al nis but conseil to virginitee.
> And for to been a wyf he yaf me leve
> of indulgence; (77–84)

(But this counsel is not taken by everyone. . . . But nonetheless though he wrote and said he wished that every person were such as he, it is nothing but a counsel to virginity. And he gave me permission of indulgence to be a wife.)

She reassures herself with Paul's own words:

> And everich hath of God a propre yifte,
> Som this, som that, as him liketh shifte. (103–4)

(And everyone has a proper gift of God, some this, some that, as it pleases him to distribute.)

However, whilst her prologue may begin with the apparent humility of seeing marriage as a second-best state, to be entered into by one who cannot live up to the perfections of virginity, within 300 lines she is joyously and positively celebrating the sexual enjoyment and fulfilment obtained through her marriages:

> But, Lord Crist! Whan that it remembreth me
> Upon my youthe, and on my jolitee,
> It tikleth me aboute myn herte roote.
> Unto this day it dooth myn herte boote
> That I have had my world as in my time. (469–73)

(But Lord Christ! When I remember about my youth and my sport, it tickles me about my heart's root. To this day it does my heart good that I have had my world in my time.)

Her obvious pleasure in the flesh would have been frowned upon by many pillars of the medieval Church, grounded as they were in notions of asceticism. As far as it goes, her 'interpretation' of St Paul is correct. He had no commandment concerning virgins, yet he believed that 'it is well for a person to remain as he is' (1 Cor. 7:25–6). It is no sin to marry, but those who marry will have 'worldly troubles' (1 Cor. 7:28). The Wife of Bath puts it thus:

> Virginitee is greet perfeccion,
> And continence eek with devocion,
> But Crist that of perfeccion is welle
> Bad nat every wight he sholde go selle
> Al that he hadde, and gyve it to the poore

And in swich wise folwe him and his foore.
He spak to hem that wolde lyve parfitly. (105–11)

(Virginity is great perfection, and also continence with devotion. But Christ who is the source of perfection did not command every man that he ought to go sell all that he had, and give it to the poor, and in such a fashion follow him and his footsteps. He spoke to those who would live perfectly.)

Her evasion of the precept from Matt. 19:21 seems reasonable enough, for ideas of human perfection had to be tempered with an understanding view of mankind, who is subject to original sin, and thus to ignorance and concupiscence. Perfection for the Christian was relative, and because the various means whereby perfection might be cultivated – prayer, poverty, virginity – are the ways of an ascetic, the notion of degrees or grades of perfection developed.

This principle of grades lies behind the Church's attitude to marriage in the Middle Ages. The three grades of chastity were marriage, widowhood and virginity, and their relative merits have already been outlined in Chapter 2. Marriage was a righteous state and permissible, but less meritorious than virginity. Widowhood stood somewhere in between. Each state gave different rates of return in terms of spiritual investment. John Mirk, writing about 1400, expressed this notion thus in his sermon on the feast-day of the Assumption of the Blessed Virgin:

This wall þat ys þe ordyr of maydenhod, ys passyng hegh; for þeras hit ys well kepte, hit ys herre þen wedloke, hit ys her þen widow-hod, and hath worschip yn Heuen passyng all oþer. (Mirk, p. 230)

(This wall that is the order of virginity is passing high, for wherever it is well kept, it is higher than wedlock, it is higher than widowhood and is honoured in heaven above all others.)

St Augustine had written that, although marriage was not condemned, it was not desirable for a widow to remarry. It was likewise more desirable in marriage that 'even during the life of her husband, by his consent, a female vow continence unto Christ' (Augustine of Hippo, *De Bono Vid.*, xiii). In his treatise on virginity, St Augustine had held up the chaste marriage of the Virgin Mary as an example of the way in which married persons may live most perfectly (Augustine of Hippo, *De Sancta Virg.*, iv). Alice, the Wife of Bath, refers to this suggestion without enthusiasm:

> . . . if that he and she
> Wolde leden al hir lyf in chastitee (93–4),

and January in Chaucer's *Merchant's Tale* rejects it completely. He could not live *in chastitee ful holily* with his prospective bride (1455). Chaucer's *Second Nun's Tale*, however, tells of Cecilia and Valerian, who did indeed vow themselves to such a chaste marriage. Theirs is a marriage more ideal than any other in *The Canterbury Tales*, and turns out to be a prelude to martyrdom.

Assuming that one had decided to embark on this state of third-rate perfection, and that one could anticipate an average marital relationship with one's spouse, the reasons why one should contemplate marriage were clearly laid down. St Paul said: 'But because of the temptation to immorality, each man should have his own wife and each woman her own husband' (1 Cor. 7:2). *Hali Meidenhad*, with somewhat more exaggeration, in line with its author's determination to convince his audience that virginity was best, presented wedlock as legalized by the Church as a bed for the sick to catch the feeble. In their headlong fall to the lechers' punishment in hell, these weak-willed people were 'halted in wedlock, and softly alighted in the bed of its law' (*Hali Meidenhad*, 281–9). Marriage properly approached could be regarded as a remedy against lust. Chaucer's Parson in his Tale, which is really a treatise on the seven deadly sins, deals with marriage under the heading Remedy against the Sin of Lust:

> Trewe effect of marriage clenseth fornicacioun and replenysseth hooly Chirch of good lynage; for that is the end of marriage. (Chaucer, p. 258)

The author of *Hali Meidenhad* could find no scriptural support for arguments *against* marriage, against what he called

> that same indecent burning of the flesh, that same flaming itch of carnal lust . . . that beastly copulation, that shameless coition, that foulness of stinking ordure and uncomely deed. (*Hali Meidenhad*, 108–11)

The 'loathsome act' is 'in wedlock someways to be tolerated'. A couple does not rot in the filth of sexual licence, provided 'they lawfully hold to their wedlock' (*Hali Meidenhad*, 174–5).

St Ambrose and St Jerome could be marshalled to show that one must marry for the purpose of procreation, otherwise one's lustful motives made one an adulterer (Ambrose, *Luke*, I, xliii–xlvi, and Jerome, *Ephesians*, III, v, 22–3). To prevent procreation by contraception or abortion made one, according to St Augustine, a female whore or a male adulterer (Noonan, 1973, p. 424, citing Gratian's reference to Augustine of Hippo, *De Nuptiis*, I, xv). For most medieval theologians the chief, though not the only, end of marriage was the procreation of children. Fidelity was also an important component of marriage, the second of the 'goods of marriage' which originated with St Augustine (Augustine of Hippo, *De Bono Con.*, iv). The third 'good' was the *sacramentum*, and this was what marriage *is*, the indissoluble union between husband and wife which reflected the love between Christ and the Church. St Augustine enjoined husband and wife to love each other, not as spouses, but as creatures of God. Yet he considers also a union which involves sexual intercourse 'not through desire of children, but through glow of lust' to be a true marriage, because lust has been 'brought under a lawful bond' (*De Bono Con.*, v). Gratian steered his way through the arguments of Ambrose, Jerome and Augustine to state that if two people experienced marital affection, even if they made love out of lust rather than the desire to have children, then they *were* spouses, and not fornicators (Noonan, 1973, p. 425, citing Gratian, cols 1119–25). For husband and wife to make love 'for the satisfying of lust' was to

Augustine a venial fault, 'by reason of the faith of the bed' (Augustine of Hippo, *De Bono Con.*, vi).

Extra-marital or pre-marital sex was naturally frowned upon, but even within marriage, rules and reasons for inter-course were laid down. Spouses could not make love during times of penance such as Lent and Advent, nor on Saturdays, in preparation for the Lord's Day, nor on the eves of feast-days. The uncleanness associated with sex is here apparent. Amongst the eighth set of Questions asked of Pope Gregory by St Augustine of Canterbury, according to the Venerable Bede, are the following: 'And may a man enter Church after relations with his wife before he has washed? Or receive the sacred mystery of Communion?' Pope Gregory's reply ran thus:

It is not fitting that a man who has approached his wife should enter Church before he has washed, nor is he to enter at once, though washed. The ancient Law prescribed that man in such cases should wash, and forbade him to enter a holy place before sunset. But this may be understood spiritually, for when a man's mind is attracted to those pleasures by lawless desire, he should not regard himself as fitted to join in Christian worship until these heated desires cool in the mind, and he has ceased to labour under wrongful passions. And although various nations have differing views on this matter and observe different customs, it was always the ancient Roman usage for such a man to seek purification, and out of reverence to refrain awhile from entering a holy place. In making this observation we do not condemn marriage itself, but since lawful intercourse must be accompanied by bodily pleasure, it is fitting to refrain from entering a holy place, since desire itself is not blameless. (Bede, I, 27)

Robert Mannynge of Brunne rhymed the advice in his early-fourteenth-century *Handlyng Synne*:

> ȝyf þou euer þy wyfe lay by
> Yn tyme of penaunce, to seye flesshly,
> ȝyf þou be custumable þarto
> Þou synnest gretly, my boke seyþ so.
> Yn holy tyme, and halyday

Forbere þy wife, ȝyf þat þou may. . . .
Yn lenten tyme of fastyng
Shalt þou leue to do swyche þyng,
Yn estyr tyme also, y forbede
Þat þou haunte any swyche dede. (2009–24)

(If you ever lay by your wife, that is carnally, in time of penance, if you are in the habit of doing so, you sin greatly, my book says so. In holy time and holy day, abstain from your wife if you can. . . . In Lenten time of fasting, you must forsake doing such a thing. In Easter time also I forbid you to perform any such deed.)

Even when no such restraints as those in regard to 'time of penance' were being imposed, yet other moral hurdles were erected for unwary couples. Chaucer's Parson set out the four reasons for which a man and his wife may have sexual union: the first is for procreation; the second is in order that each spouse should render to the other his bodily debt 'for neither of them hath power of his owene body'. This is the *debitum* of St Paul, which occurs as 'due reverence' in the Authorized Version. The third reason for intercourse is to avoid lechery, and the fourth is deadly sin.

The first reason is clear enough, and has been mentioned above. Pope Gregory's answer to Augustine of Canterbury (part of which has been already quoted) continues: 'Lawful intercourse should be for the procreation of offspring and not for mere pleasure; to obtain children, and not to satisfy lust'. A man moved to make love to his wife only out of desire for children need not, according to Gregory, be debarred from entering church, or from receiving Holy Communion.

But when lust takes the place of desire for children, the pair have cause for regret; and although the holy teachings give them permission, this carries a warning with it. For when the apostle Paul said 'whoever cannot contain let him marry' he added 'This I say by way of permission not as a command'. This concession makes it lawful, yet not good; so that when he spoke of permission, he indicated that it was not good. (Bede, I, 27)

The second reason for which a married couple is permitted to indulge in sexual intercourse also stems from a statement from St Paul, though it seems to represent something between procreation and lust which Pope Gregory did not appear to recognize in his dealings with Augustine of Canterbury:

> The husband should give to his wife her conjugal rights, and likewise the wife to her husband. For the wife does not rule over her own body, but the husband does. Likewise the husband does not rule over his own body, but the wife does. (1 Cor. 7:3–4)

Begetting children and paying the marriage debt were generally recognized as 'meritorious' reasons for making love. The wife

> hath merite of chastitee that yeldeth to hire husbonde the dette of hire body, ye, though it be agayn hir likyng and the lust of hir herte. (Chaucer, p. 259)

(has the merit of chastity who yields the debt of her body to her husband, yes, though it is contrary to her liking and the desire of her heart.)

Thus says Chaucer's Parson, and his failure to render the full meaning of Paul's statement on the reciprocal demands of the marriage debt may reflect a profound disquiet about the woman's role in sexual intercourse. A celibate's uneasy disapproval of a sexually demanding woman would not have been allayed by Dame Alice of Bath's approach to this very subject:

> Yn wyfhod I wol use myn instrument
> As frely as my Makere hath it sent.
> If I be daungerous, God yeve me sorwe!
> Myn housbonde shal it have bothe eve and morwe
> Whan that him list come forth and paye his dette. (149–53)

(In wifehood I intend to use my instrument as generously as my maker has sent it. If I am niggardly, may God give me sorrow! My husband shall have it morning and night when it pleases him to come forth and pay his debt.)

For her, paying the marital debt is to be a matter of regular toil and service from her husband. He will be a *dettour and a thral* (155). Soon afterwards she rejoices:

As help me God, I laughe when I thinke
How pitously a-night I made hem swinke [toil]! (201–2)

It could be argued that the Wife gives a clearer definition here of the marriage debt than that provided by many medieval theologians, but of course she too neglects the mutual obligation involved.

The Parson explains that to make love in order to avoid lechery, presumably with some third party (his third reason) is a venial sin, and adds: *Trewely scarsly may any of thise be withoute venial sinne, for the corrupcion and for the delit* (Chaucer, p. 259).

The fourth reason for which man and wife may assemble is *oonly for amorous love*, and this is a mortal sin to the Parson. It seems likely that a large number of married couples would have found it impossible to exclude amorous love from entering into the act of paying their mutual debt or avoiding lechery. To contrive to make love without either joy or passion would appear to be the direction of the Parson's exhortations, for the degree of sin involved in intercourse seems to be directly related to the degree of pleasure deriving from it. Such a viewpoint seems to have moved away from Gratian's charitable conclusions mentioned earlier. Earlier Patristic attitudes to sex were caught up in the thirteenth century in the new study of Aristotle, for whom rationalism and contemplation were to be valued above all else. Sexual orgasm, because it momentarily overcomes rational thought, made many respected writers, of whose views the Parson is only a late reflection, extremely nervous about the rightness of such pleasure. Such rationalism in an approach to marriage does not entirely fit the facts of human sexuality, and the Wife of Bath in her own vital way appears as an earthy voice attempting to set the record just a little bit straighter. In the process, she makes her own jibe at the explanations and arguments of ingenious and desperate theologians:

Telle me also, to what conclusion
Were membres maad of generacion

And of so parfit wys a wight ywroght?
Trusteth right wel, they were nat maad for noght.
Glose whoso wole and seye bothe up and doun
That they were maked for purgacioun
Of uryne, and oure bothe thynges smale
Were eek to knowe a femele from a male,
And for noon oother cause, ...
So that the clerkes be nat with me wrothe,
I sey this, that they maked ben for bothe,
This is to seye, for office and for ese
Of engendrure, there we nat God displese. (115–28)

(Tell me besides, for what purpose were reproductive organs made? And in so perfect a manner a [little] thing made? Depend full well, they were not made for nothing. Whoever likes to explain it, and whatever arguments they may put forward [to the effect] that they were made for the excretion of urine, and that both our little things were also in order to distinguish a female from a male and for no other reason, ... Provided clerics are not angry with me I say this, that they are made for both, that is for service and for the pleasure of procreation, in which we do not displease God.)

How, she demands, could a man pay his wife her debt 'if he did not use his blessed instrument?' Her practical approach to sex is coupled, however, with a determination to dominate her spouse by fair means or by foul, and this makes her the very kind of woman the anti-feminists loved to hate.

Anti-feminism was as old as classical antiquity, and the view of woman as an inferior being begun by the pagan Greeks was carefully preserved, indeed intensified by Christian writers from Tatian in the second-century onwards. This literary tradition was preserved into the Middle Ages, carefully nurtured by references to the Church Fathers, buttressed by quotations from the Bible, and where necessary from pagan Latin writers also. The Wife of Bath may easily be seen as the anti-feminists' nightmare wife, brash, talkative, lecherous, show-off, a bullyer and tormentor of her husband(s), wasteful of their money on clothes and personal adornment. In fact, a more obvious compendium of women's vices presented in garrulous female form would be difficult to find in medieval literature. The literary conceit of anti-feminism was most ably carried forward by preachers in the Middle Ages:

> To the vast mass of the middle and lower orders for whom no romantic minstrelsy had provided a chivalrous ideal, the pulpit, their one oracle of learning and refinement, presented a picture of womanhood, ill-balanced indeed, but sufficiently realistic and lively to appeal to the lay mind. Thus early there grew up in popular verse a traditional satire, half-comic, half-tragic, from which neither the greatest of medieval English poets nor the greatest of all our dramatists could escape in their day, and one that stubbornly persists through the literature of following centuries to that of modern times. (Owst, p. 377)

The source of this anti-feminist stream in English literature was certainly nourished by the writings of medieval preachers and theologians:

> Where healthy human nature seems to demand some positive doctrine of sexual happiness, [the preachers] speak only . . . of sin and temptation, of forbidden pleasures and lusts, of needful fears and repressions, haunted by the same old shadow of Original Sin, the same primitive ascetical ideals of their ancestors. (Owst, p. 377).

And the butt of all these fears and repressions was womankind. Chaucer's Chaunticleer in the *Nonnes Prestes Tale*, echoing the thirteenth-century author of the *Speculum Laicorum*, tells his favourite hen dame Pertilote that *Mulier est hominis confusio*. Chaunticleer's translation of his Latin,

> Madame, the sentence [meaning] of this Latyn is,
> 'Womman is mannes joye and al his blis' (3165–6),

condescends at once to her vanity and her ignorance, compounding the insult. Woman's beauty was a snare, an outward form of little duration 'a withered flower, carnal felicity, human concupiscence' (Owst, p. 48). Ecclus. 9:8 warned:

Turn away your eyes from a shapely woman, and do not look
intently at beauty belonging to another; for many have been
mislead by a woman's beauty and by it passion is kindled like fire.

Bromyard, a fourteenth-century Dominican, in his *Summa
Praedicantium* speaks of the vileness which men would perceive if
their eyes could penetrate the entrails of beautiful women
(Bromyard, II, s.v. *Pulchrit.*). This was really part of the
broader homiletic approach which sought to denounce every
form of outward show which cloaked the spiritual reality
beneath. The pessimism about all earthly beauty is particularly
troubling in the discussion of matrimony by medieval homilists. Woman was not believed to be capable of intellectual
accomplishments, yet the beauty and ornament which were
expected of her in lieu of rational thought and behaviour were
most cruelly used to her detriment.

St Jerome was one of the most influential heirs to the age-old
literary tradition of anti-feminism, and he produced many
bitterly satirical attacks on the absurdities of women's licen-
tiousness, gluttony, ostentation in dress and make-up. His deep
and sincere emotional attachment to asceticism made him treat
marriage with violent and extravagant revulsion, and his complaints against women were presented with his undoubtedly
brilliant powers of observation and description. Perhaps it was
this brilliance of description which made him an attractive
source of anti-feminist ideas to a poet like Geoffrey Chaucer.
Jerome's views on marriage contained in the *Epistola adversus
Jovinianum* most certainly drew on earlier anti-feminist works by
Aristotle, Plutarch, Seneca and Theophrastus, though all but
Plutarch's *Praecepta Coniugalia* are now lost. The Wife of Bath's
fifth husband, Jankin the clerk, seems to have owned a volume
which contained 'Valerie and Theophraste' – the *Epistola
Valerii ad Rufinum de non Ducenda Uxore* of Walter Map and the
Liber de Nuptiis of Theophrastus – and in addition the work of a
clerk at Rome,

> A cardinal, that highte [was called] Seint Jerome
> That made a book agayn Jovinian. (673–5)

There could be no clearer indication that Dame Alice is herself cast as a direct literary descendant of the Christian satirists' Woman, the woman 'loud and wayward' of Prov. 7:10–12.

For Theophrastus and Jerome, a fair woman soon finds lovers; even if she is ugly, it is easy for her to be wanton. In such a climate of opinion, no woman can find favour. A beautiful woman is troublesome to guard because many men desire her. Eustache Deschamps in his *Miroir de Mariage* presents the true friend's advice against marriage no less mordantly than St Jerome:

> Se tu la prens, qu'elle soit belle
> Tu n'aras jamais paix a elle
> Car chascuns la couvoitera
> Et dure chose a toy sera
> De garder ce que un chascun voite. (1625–9)

(If you take her, if she is beautiful, you will never have peace from her, because everyone will covet her, and it will be a difficult thing for you to keep what everyone else is hankering after.)

Deschamps does not make any attempt to deny the ancestry of his theme, and uses both Juvenal and Herodotus to buttress his arguments. Herodotus maintained that a woman had no shame at all, and Juvenal that no woman was chaste if pursued and pressed hard enough. In spite of the trouble caused by a beautiful woman, an ugly woman is not worth having, although Jerome maintains that 'the misery of having an ugly wife is less than that of keeping watch on a beautiful one' (Jerome, *Ad Jov.* I, xlvii).

If a woman cannot be desired for her beauty, then perhaps her talents at housekeeping should cause her to be valued. January in Chaucer's *Merchant's Tale* quotes 'Theophraste' and his uncomplimentary remarks in order to dismiss them:

> 'Ne take no wyf', quod he, 'for housbondrye,
> As for to spare in houshold thy dispence.
> A trewe servant dooth moore diligence
> Thy good to kepe, than thyn owene wyf,
> For she wol clayme half part al hir lyf'. (1296–1300)

('Do not take a wife', said he, 'for economy, so as to save your expenditure in the household. A loyal servant works harder to take care of your property than your own wife, for she will claim a half-share all her life'.)

Jerome had written:

> If it is because of the management of the house, the comforts of fatigue, and the flight from loneliness that one marries: then a faithful servant who is obedient to his master's judgment and obeys his arrangements is much better than a wife who thinks herself to be the mistress of that place, who, if she sets her mind against that of her husband, it is because it pleases her, and not because she is ordered to do so. (Jerome, *Ad Jov.* I, xlvii)

So much for housekeeping. And as a warmer of the matrimonial couch, woman is also worthless. Indeed her love is worse than worthless. The Wife of Bath recasts Jerome's sentiments thus, in a reconstructed speech to one of her husbands:

> Thou liknest eek wommenes love to helle,
> To bareyne lond, ther water may nat dwelle.
> Thou liknest it also to wilde fyr;
> The moore it brenneth, the moore it hath desir
> To consume every thyng that brent wole be.
> Thou seyest, right as wormes shende a tree,
> Right so a wyf destroyeth hire housbonde;
> This knowe they that been to wyves bonde. (371–8)

(You liken woman's love to hell, to barren land where water cannot live. You compare it also to wild fire; the more it burns the more it desires to consume everything that will be burnt. You say, just as worms destroy a tree, exactly the same way a wife destroys her husband. Those who are bound to wives know this.)

Jerome, making it clear that he is drawing on the wisdom of Solomon in Prov. 30:16, which avers that woman's love is one of three insatiable things, states that he is speaking of the love of women in general, not just the love of harlots or adulteresses:

> Here, not the harlot, nor the adulteress is spoken of but the love of women in general I accuse, which is always insatiable, which once

extinguished is inflamed, and after abundance again is poor, renders the spirit of man effeminate, and once roused to passion allows no thought of anything else. [Jerome, *Ad Jov.* I, xxviii]

If Alice is an opponent of St Jerome's outlook, Justinus in the *Merchant's Tale* proves himself a worthy disciple of the satirist. Justinus predicts that January's future wife, May, may prove to be her husband's purgatory. He also echoes St Jerome's anecdote of a Roman nobleman when he adverts to the pain of his own marriage:

> . . . my neighebores aboute
> And namely of wommen many a route
> Seyn that I have the moost stedefast wyf,
> And eek the mekest oon that bereth lyf;
> But I woot best where wryngeth me my sho. (1549–53)

(My neighbours round about and especially many a group of women say that I have the most steadfast wife, and also the meekest one alive; but I know best where my shoe pinches.)

It would appear then, that to the anti-feminist, woman was not to be valued for her beauty, nor for her love, nor for her good housekeeping.

A great many English homilists of the thirteenth and fourteenth centuries seem to have found no need to preach any belief in the joy of earthly love, and their view of human love is as gross and materialistic as that of Chaucer's Merchant, to whom all love was lust, whether inside or outside wedlock. The preacher of MS Harley 2398, folio 98b, quoted by Owst (p. 382) had no great opinion of love-making. There was as much poison in *kyssyng and grypying and beholding* of the apparently harmless sort as in

> spekyng and in takyng hede to wyckede and unclene speches, and in other unlawesom [unlawful] touchynges onlyche [only] by shrewed [depraved] delectacioun, and in other lecherous fykelynges [flatteries] and ragyngs [wanton pursuits].

Another homilist in the same manuscript could be seen as deriving his abhorrence of the *lecherous speche of women and kyssynges and nyce contenance-making* firmly from St Paul's first letter to the Corinthians 7:1, 'Now concerning the matters about which you wrote. It is well for a man not to touch a woman'. However, modern scholarship would see this not as Paul's own statement, but as a restatement of a question to which he is about to reply (Caird, p. 275). Marriage to the anti-feminist preacher and to the poet in anti-feminist guise appears as a perennial curbing of lust born of daily dealings with a teasing woman, a penance which can only be interrupted in order to undertake the task of continuing the human race. Bromyard in the fourteenth century speaks as slightingly of marriage as did St Jerome in the fourth. Marriage is full of anxieties, discomforts and dangers. There is no possibility that a wife can bring joy. Sterility is a problem, fecundity is a problem. Beauty has to be guarded, and a lovely wife is bound to be vain and extravagant, always needing money to spend on herself. It is likely, as Owst suggested (p. 386), that the ground base of medieval attacks on the evil of women is not to be found in St Paul at all, but may be found in the Book of Proverbs 7:10–12. It speaks of a woman

> dressed as a harlot, wily of heart.
> She is loud and wayward,
> her feet do not stay at home;
> now in the street, now in the market,
> and at every corner she lies in wait.

Two of the most famous female characters in medieval literature, Noah's wife in the Miracle Plays and Chaucer's Wife of Bath, can probably be traced to this most distinguished ancestor. The Wife of Bath certainly liked to get about. The pilgrim narrator's innocent comment that she *koude (knew) muchel of wandryng by the weye* (*Gen. Prologue*, 467) looks not only to her many pilgrimages, but also to her varied experiences of love. She had *passed many a straunge strem* and also *koude of that art (love) the olde daunce* (*Gen. Prologue*, 464 and 476). She makes no secret of her desire to get out of the house. Her husband might well complain, as she says in the Prologue to her Tale, that like a cat with a sleek coat

> She wol nat dwelle in house half a day,
> But forth she wole, er any day be dawed
> To shewe hir skyn, and goon a-caterwawed.
> This is to seye, if I be gay, sire shrewe,
> I wol renne out, my borel for to shewe. (352–6)

(She does not wish to remain in the house half a day, but wishes to go forth long before daybreak to show her skin and go caterwauling. This is to say, if I be lively, Sir Shrew, I will run out, to show my coarse woolen clothes.)

A sermon quoted by Owst (p. 119) cites the sinfulness of *nyce maydens* who display themselves in dancing and singing and walking about in meadows in order to lose their virginity, *ffor it byfalleth to maydenes to be in stilnesse and in cloose, as oure lady seynte Marie was whenne the angel come to hure*. The fate of Dinah, Jephthah's daughter, who wandered from her home to visit someone and was raped, was held up as an example of what can happen to an errant woman (Owst, p. 119). Another scriptural passage which helped to give rise to and in turn was used to buttress the homilist's view of the wandering woman is found in St Paul's first letter to Timothy 5:13, when he speaks of women who are 'idlers, gadding about from house to house, and not only idlers but gossips and busybodies, saying what they should not'. Robert Mannynge of Brunne's *Handlyng Synne* is also fiercely disapproving of

> Wymmen þat go fro strete to strete,
> One or ouþer for to mete,
> Of pryde comþ swyche desyre,
> For þey haue on hem feyre atyre:
> But she wul to þe prest þat telle,
> She may þerfore go to helle. (3449–54)

(Women who go from street to street to meet one another, such desire comes of pride, because they are wearing fine clothes. Unless she tells it to the priest, she may go to hell for it.)

For the Wife of Bath, her ideal husband is one who will tell her to go where she pleases and enjoy herself, and he will believe no stories:

> We love no man that taketh kep or charge
> Wher that we goon; we wol ben at our large. (321–2)

(We love no man who exercizes careful watch over where we go: we wish to enjoy complete freedom.)

Female garrulousness is well illustrated in the 856 lines of the prologue to Dame Alice's Tale. Women were well known for wishing to *rowne togedyr* (whisper) in church instead of listening to the sermon, while 'the fiend sat on their shoulders writing on a long roll as fast as he could' (Owst, pp. 176–7). Not surprisingly there is an *old Englysh sawe*, quoted by John Mirk in his *Festial*, that *a mayde schulde be seen but not herd* (p. 230). Woman's tendency to chatter could be traced back to Eve's garrulousness in the garden of Eden. By her willingness to engage the fiend in conversation, she revealed her weakness to him, and gave him an opportunity to bring her to ruin. The ideal of Mary, always to be set against Eve, could be used as a corrective even in this, for her speech is recorded in the gospel a scant four times. Mirk in his sermon on the feast of the Assumption notes these four occasions:

> ons to Gabryell, the secunde to Elyzabeth, þe þryd to her sonne yn þe tempyll, þe fourþe at þe weddyng yn the Cane of Galyle. (Mirk, *Festial*, p. 230)

(Once to Gabriel, the second to Elizabeth, the third to her son in the temple, the fourth at the wedding in Cana of Gallilee.)

He cites St Bernard of Clairvaux as his authority for this, and claims not that they are merely the four *recorded* utterances of Mary, but that they represent the sum total of words that Mary spoke *in alle hyr lyfe*, an ideal which even the most taciturn of women could hardly hope to emulate.

Closely allied to woman's desire to roam about and chat to her friends is her vanity in dress. Says Jerome:

> Many are the things that must be used by one's wife – valuable clothes, gold, jewels, extravagant things, servants, various articles of furniture, litters and edibles. (Jerome, PL XXIII, 276)

What sey ʒe men of ladys pryde, writes Robert Mannynge of Brunne,

> þat gone trayling ouer syde:
> ʒif a lady were ryghtly shreue
> Better hyt were in almes ʒeue
> To soule helpe hyt myʒt do bote,
> þat trayleþ lowe undyr þe fote.
> Wymples, kerchyues, saffrund betyde,
> ʒelugh vnder ʒelugh þay hyde;
> þan wete men neuer, wheþer ys wheþer
> þe ʒelugh wymple or þe leþer. (3439–48)

(What do you men say of ladies' pride, that go trailing (in long trains) far and wide: If a lady were properly shriven it would be better to give alms; (the money spent on) that which trails underfoot could be used as a help for souls. Wimples, kerchiefs (are) sometimes coloured saffron. They hide yellow skin under yellow cloth; then men never know which is which, the yellow wimple or the skin.)

The Jealous Husband in the *Roman de la Rose* (44: 9079–360) speaks of the gilded bands and head-dresses, the golden ring, the jewelry, sapphires, rubies, emeralds and pearls which make a wife proud of such seeming worth. Such decorations are an encouragement to admirers. He determines as follows:

> I'll take away all these deceitful clothes
> That lead to fornication and naught else,
> And then you'll go no more to show yourself
> And lure the ribalds to adultery.

The image of singeing the cat's fur as a means of making her stay at home is often used to suggest a way of dealing with a dressy, wandering woman, and may well have been a homilist's commonplace. Many and furious were the attacks on women's love of finery in the writings of medieval preachers. For the Dominican, John Bromyard, the fine Easter weather, coming after the physical hardships of winter as well as the spiritual rigours of Lent, signalled a time for pageants, games and feasting at which a woman could dress up in her finest and most fashionable clothes, and win back all the newly repentant sinners of the Lenten period for the devil (Bromyard, I, s.v. *Bellum*, and II, s.v. *Ornatus*). He calls dressed-up, dancing, frolicking women the 'devil's packhorses, who put themselves up for sale', sinners whose 'feet run to evil', and who are to be shunned like the woman in Ecclus. 9:4:

> Do not associate with a woman singer,
> lest you be caught in her intrigues.

The Wife of Bath with her Sunday head-dress weighing ten pounds, her stockings of *fyn scarlet reed*, and her shoes *ful moyste and newe* was as ostentatiously dressy as any anti-feminist preacher could have imagined, and to display herself is not at all to her disliking:

> In al the parisshe wif ne was ther noon
> That to the offryng bifore hire shold goon,
> And if there dide, certeyn so wrooth was she
> That she was out of alle charitee. (*Gen. Prologue*, 449–52)

(There was no woman in the entire parish who was to go to the offering before her. And if (one) did, indeed she was so angry, that she lost all her love of her neighbour.)

A wife's tendency to berate her innocent but long suffering spouse is detailed as far back as Ecclus. 26:6:

> There is grief of heart and sorrow
> when a wife is envious of a rival,
> and a tongue-lashing makes it known to all.

It is alluded to by St Jerome in his letter against Jovinian:

> Then throughout the whole night there are garrulous questions: in public she must come out more adorned than others, all these things must be venerated by everyone, and I am despised in the miserable company of women. Why were you looking at our neighbour? Of what were you speaking to the servant girl? Coming from the forum what did you bring with you? We are not allowed to have an ally, not even an acquaintance . . . her face must always be noticed, her beauty praised: if you were to look at another she would think you displeased. . . . (Jerome, *Ad Jov.* I, xlvii)

Noah's wife in the Miracle Play cycles is a shrewish performer. In the Towneley play of *Noah*, she wades in to attack Noah without any obvious provocation:

> For thou art alway adred, be it fals or trew,
> > But God knowes I am led – and that may I rew –
> Full ill;
> For I dar be thi borow
> From euen vnto morow
> Thou spekis euer of sorow;
> God send the onys thi fill. (201–7)

(For you are always afraid, be it false or true, but God knows I am led, and that I may regret, very bitterly; For I dare be your pledge from evening unto morrow, you always speak of sorrow, God send you your fill for once.)

All bad husbands should be cursed, she feels, and makes no secret of the fact that she thinks Noah fits into this category. Yet she seems to know how to get her own way with him:

> Bot yit otherwhile,
> What with gam and with gyle
> I shall smyte and smyle,
> And qwite hym his mede. (213–16)

(But some other time, what with trick and guile, I shall strike and smile, and give him his just desserts.)

The Wife of Bath's abilities in the area of 'tongue-lashing' are well documented out of her own mouth. At the end of her disclosures she can claim:

> Lordings, right thus, as ye have understonde,
> Baar I stifly myne olde housbondes on honde
> That thus they seyden in hir dronkenesse; . . .
> O Lord! the peyne I dide hem and the wo,
> Ful giltelees, by Goddes sweet pine. (379–85)

(Gentlemen, just so as you have understood, I boldly deluded my old husbands that they spoke thus when they were drunk . . . O Lord! the suffering and misery I caused them, though they were completely innocent, by God's sweet torment!)

It is hardly surprising to discover that wives capable of such villainy as overdressing, garrulity, wandering about the town and putting themselves in the way of lovers, could be beaten. Just as errant daughters who stood out against their parents' matrimonial plans for them could be and were severely chastized, a woman, once married, could be beaten for not conforming to her husband's ideas about her behaviour. Not only could she be beaten for a major transgression like adultery, but also for bearing her husband a mentally-handicapped child (Gautier, p. 350). It was clearly an advance towards more humane behaviour when Phillippe de Beaumanoir, in his thirteenth-century *Coutumes de Beauvaisis*, declared that a man should only beat his wife 'within reason' (Beaumanoir, p. 335, 1631). Coulton quotes St Bernadine of Siena, who was writing shortly after Chaucer's death, as saying that there is need for moderation in wife-beating; those who beat their wives because they speak 'a word more than they like' are called 'raving madmen'. Bernadine goes on: 'Consider, rascal, consider the noble fruit of thy wife, and have patience; it is not right to beat her for every cause, no!' However, in another sermon he isolates extravagant and immodest dressing as a reason for beating a wife 'with feet and fists' (Coulton, 1950, pp. 190–1).

In the fifteenth-century *Book of the Knight of the Tower*, written for the education of his daughters, the Knight takes up a great deal of space treating of the proper behaviour of a wife towards her husband. She must never argue or quarrel with him in public, but courteously tell him his faults on a more convenient- ly private occasion (p. 129). Two chapters further on he cites the example of St Elizabeth, who *drad and doubted* her husband. She always spoke so courteously to him that he could never be angry with her. A diplomatic mixture of fear and love seems to be required in the attitude of a wife to her husband, for the woman who behaves otherwise can be beaten. The Knight goes on to tell his daughters of the wife of a burgess who answered her husband so *noiously and shamefully to fore the peple* that in his anger he

> smote her with his fyste to the erthe and smote her with his foote on the vysage so that he brake her nose by which she was euer after al disfygured. (p. 35)

In the *General Prologue* to the *Canterbury Tales* we are told that the Wife of Bath *was somdel deef, and that was scathe* (was somewhat deaf and that was a pity, 446), and later, in the prologue to her Tale, Alice gives us a clue about her deafness: because she tore three pages out of her fifth husband's precious book of anti- feminist writings, he struck her on the head with his fist, so that she lay on the floor as though dead (788–812). However, this royal row of theirs seemed to have been a means of bringing them to a near-perfect understanding, in the Wife's view, because in his remorse, Jankin gave her the control of house and land, his tongue and hand, *and* burned his book into the bargain. The Knight of the Tower tells the story of a wager amongst three merchants as to whose wife was most obedient. When the first two find their wives at fault for not obeying a strange command without query, they have no compunction in beating them. The wife of the third is a model of obedience, and the Knight concludes

> And thus ought every good woman to fere and obeye her lord and husbonde and to doo his commaundement, is hit right or wrong,

yf the commaundement be not ouer outrageous. And yf ther be vyce therin she is not to blame but the blame abydeth vpon her lord and husbonde. (p. 37)

This seems to be carrying wifely obedience beyond what was acceptable even to the Church, and is also somewhat puzzling as to what command might be more 'outrageous' than 'sinful'.

Whether one is dealing with the rather theoretical notions of women emanating from the writings of St Jerome in the fourth century or John Bromyard in the fourteenth, or with the more 'realistic' pictures of the shrewish wife drawn by the poets and dramatists, the general view of woman provided by the anti-feminists is of a creature who is a necessary plague to the better half of mankind. She is tolerated because of her essential function of continuing the species. The only really worthwhile role which a woman can play in marriage is thus seen to be that of producing offspring in fear and obedience to her lord and husband. All other aspects of her activities in marriage seem to be treated with varying degrees of ridicule, fear and loathing. The view of men which emerges from such writings is not very flattering either. They present themselves as narrow-minded, short-sighted, insecure bullies, who take delight in keeping women in a properly subservient place, by main force if necessary.

That all wives did not behave as the anti-feminists would have us believe is an obvious judgement to arrive at; equally, it has to be seen that all husbands could not possibly have been anti-feminist bullies. January's statement in the *Merchant's Tale*, that *mariage is a ful grete sacrament*, is no less true for being ironic in its context. St Bernard of Clairvaux, whose writings on love can compare with those of any poet of the twelfth century, seems to have preferred to symbolize the love of God for the human soul by the love between man and woman, both in his long commentary on the Song of Songs as well as in other writings on the love of God. He used the vocabulary of human love mixed with that of chivalry and war to show God's love for his Church and for the human soul (Leclercq, 1979, pp. 101–3).

He could not have done this if he had not seen human love as having a worth and validity in its own right. Nicole Oresme (c.1320–82), who ended his days as bishop of Lisieux, concerned himself with the love and friendship which should exist between husband and wife. In his translation of a commentary on the Pseudo-Economics of Aristotle, *Le Livre de Yconomique d'Aristote*, Oresme insisted that the husband is master of the household and head of his wife, but he also believed that a wife would obey and behave herself only if she could feel that her husband loved and revered her. She was to be treated as a companion, not as a servant, and she must see that her husband cared for her above all others. His respect must show itself in everything he does for her and with her. Fidelity is thus of paramount importance; if he is faithful and attentive, she will be loving and loyal in return. Oresme provided no hard and fast rules about sexual abstinence or activity for spouses, but he made it plain that there was a need for an 'art of love' between spouses without excessive demands, without abuse and rough treatment, and characterized by refinement. A husband must so satisfy his wife by his decent and honourable conduct that she will not desire to look for love elsewhere (Parmisano, I, pp. 601–2).

It is precisely as a love-bond that we like to think of marriage today, yet that there is nothing specially original or modern about such a view, is shown by attitudes like those of St Bernard and Nicole Oresme. Such views were well within a traditional attitude of the Church, for the characteristic definition of the *sacramentum*, the indissoluble bond of marriage, as indicative of the love of Christ for his Church, reflects one of the Church's most basic beliefs about the marriage bond. It stems from the interpretation of the description of marriage in the Book of Genesis 2:24, quoted by St Paul in Eph. 5:31:

> For this reason a man shall leave his father and mother and be joined to his wife, and the two shall become one flesh. This mystery is a profound one, and I am saying that it refers to Christ and the Church.

In the twelfth century, Hugh of St Victor, quoting St Paul, restated the belief that a consummated marriage is 'a great sacrament in Christ and the Church' (Hugh of St Victor, *De Sac. Ch. Fid.*, II, xi, 2). Hugh's doctrine of marriage insisted on the necessity of voluntary and reciprocal love in order to establish a true sacrament, even though he acknowledged the relative weakness and passivity of women. Innocent III in his Decretal *Debitum Pastoralis Officii* (dealing with widowers who wished to become priests) spoke of the two aspects of marriage: the consent of minds, which signifies the love of God for the just soul, and the joining of bodies, which signifies the union between Christ and the Church. That this vision of marriage often became obscured by the cold and scientific Latin of the Schoolmen, theology written by and for the professional theologian, and by the rather more heated vernacular prose of some of the more enthusiastic homilists must not blind one to the fact that the ideal of conjugal love was always there, being defined, praised, or just reflected in the writings of men like St Bernard, Hugh of St Victor, St Bonaventure, St Thomas Aquinas, and Alexander of Hales. It is found in the fourteenth-century English *Book of Vices and Virtues*, a treatise on the vernacular instruction which parish priests were enjoined to cover once a quarter with their flock. Marriage is the third branch of Chastity, knitting man and woman in one flesh, so that 'they should be of one heart by true love, nor ever separate in heart or body while they live' (*Book of Vices and Virtues*, p. 245).

The good wife as well as the bad is to be found within the pages of Holy Scripture. The good wife is 'far more precious than jewels. The heart of her husband trusts in her, and he will have no lack of gain' (Prov. 31:10–11). The chapter in Proverbs goes on to give some idea of the behaviour of the good wife. She 'seeks wool and flax', she 'rises while it is yet night and provides food for her household', she 'considers a field and buys it', she 'perceives that her merchandise is profitable', and 'makes linen garments and sells them'. She 'puts her hands to the distaff' and 'looks well to the ways of her household, and does not eat the bread of idleness'. Her children 'rise up and call her blessed; her husband also, and he praises her' (Prov. 31:10–28). Old January in the *Merchant's Tale* appears to have ideas about the role of his future wife which run along the same lines. She will look after him *sik and hool* (sick and well, 1289). She *kepeth his good, and wasteth never a deel* (looks after his property and never wastes a bit, 1343). She is

> kepere of thyn housbondrye;
> Wel may the sike man biwaille and wepe,
> Ther as ther nys no wyf the hous to kepe. (1380–2)

(keeper of your household goods; well may the sick man wail and weep where there is no wife to take care of the house.)

The life of a married man is set in security:

> He may nat be deceyved, as I gesse,
> So that he werke after his wyves reed. (1356–7)

(He cannot be deceived, in my estimation, provided he works according to his wife's advice.)

Housekeeping in a big household in the Middle Ages was certainly a great burden, involving the provision of clothes and food for a large family and for all the servants, and providing entertainment for many guests as well. A good wife would undoubtedly spend less time rearing her children than she would in ordering and supervising the production of foodstuffs and clothing which could be made on the farm or manor, and also laying in stores bought at market. The women of the Paston and Stonor letters give some notion of their many chores. Christine de Pizan's *Livre des Trois Vertus* (unpublished, see McLeod, 1976, p. 178), is a treatise on the duties of women in different ranks of society, and indicates that a lady had to know all about hiring labourers, as well as the correct seasons for different operations on the farm. She had to know about crops and the suitability of different soils, the care of animals and the best markets for farm produce. That the role of the good middle-class wife was essentially the same – a provider and manager of the household – is revealed by *Le Menagier de Paris*, written by a French bourgeois towards the end of the fourteenth century for his young wife. The wife is only fifteen and the *Menagier* is an old man, and he writes the treatise so that his wife will know how to order her household and be a good wife in the event of her marrying again after his death. In addition to detailing the proper behaviour of a wife towards her husband – from giving him good food and drink, washing his feet and bringing him fresh shoes and stockings when he has been caught in the rain to making sure there are no fleas in her bed or bedroom in summertime – the *Menagier* instructs his wife in household management: she must know about gardening and fruit-growing, about farm animals as well as household pets, about hiring workmen as well as servants. She was to see to the food and clothing of her servants, and supervise their moral well-being as well as their bodily ailments (*Menagier de Paris*, I, 168–75 and II, 59 ff.). January in the *Merchant's Tale* was quite right to send his new young wife May to visit the Squire Damien on his sick bed. That Damien is sick of love for May and uses the opportunity to hand her a love-letter are circumstances not taken into account in January's calculations on the behaviour of a good wife, nor, one presumes, in those of the *Menagier* of Paris.

In terms of personal appearance and qualities, a good wife brings many joys, as the Bible tells us:

> A loyal wife rejoices her husband,
> and he will complete his years in peace. . . .
> A wife's charm delights her husband,
> and her skill puts fat on his bones.
> A silent wife is a gift of the Lord,
> and there is nothing so precious as a
>   disciplined soul.
> A modest wife adds charm to charm,
> and no balance can weigh the value
>   of a chaste soul.
> Like the sun rising in the heights

of the Lord,
so is the beauty of a good wife in
her well ordered home.
Like the shining lamp on the holy lampstand,
so is a beautiful face on a stately figure.
Like pillars of gold on a base of silver,
so are beautiful feet with a steadfast heart. (Ecclus. 26:2–18)

And Robert Mannynge of Brunne provides at least one paean of praise to the love of a good woman in holy wedlock which can be set against all the criticism of the clerics and preachers of the fourteenth century:

> For no þyng Jhesu Cryst more quemeþ
> þan loue yn wedlak þere men hyt ȝemeth;
> Ne no þyng ys to man so dere
> As wommanys loue yñ gode manere.
>
> A gode womman ys mannys blys
> þere here loue ryȝt and stedfast ys;
> þere ys no solas vndyr heuene
> Of al þat a man may neuene,
> þat shuld a man so moche glew
> As a gode womman þat loueþ trew. (1903–12)

(For nothing pleases Jesus Christ more than love in marriage where men observe it; and nothing is so dear to man as is woman's love in a proper fashion. A good woman is man's joy, when her love is proper and stèadfast; there is no solace under heaven – of everything that a man can tell of – that should cause a man so much joy as a good woman who loves faithfully.)

Part Three

Women and Letters

9
Education and Literacy

———◆———

The monastic centres established by and for women in the so-called Dark Ages were centres of knowledge and culture. Their inmates were generally valued for their learning, sometimes exerting themselves as patronesses of scholarly and literary endeavour, and often becoming revered as saints after their death. To a large extent an examination of women and education involves a continuing look at women in relation to monastic life. However, some more general considerations may also be taken into account.

Nunneries must always have had their limitations as places of education. Many writers of religious Rules from Caesarius of Arles onwards had expressly forbidden nuns to teach children. The presence of children – as of secular lodgers – was frowned on as a practice subversive of discipline. It was good for the nuns' revenues, but bad for spiritual devotion. It made a nonsense of the claustration rule, and also infringed the rules forbidding the retention of personal property. Eudes Rigaud, bishop of Rouen in the mid-thirteenth century, habitually had boys and girls removed from convents in his diocese whenever he found them. In England bishops gave in to the custom to the point of establishing age limits beyond which children could not remain in the convent, and sometimes required that a licence be obtained in order to keep them. Boys were rarely allowed to remain after the age of eight if allowed at all; girls could probably stay up to the age of fourteen depending on the local bishop (see Power, 1922, pp. 261ff.) References to girls receiving education in a convent very often turn out to mean *velandae*, girls preparing to take the veil, not secular scholars. The children who did come to nunneries were invariably members of the upper, and wealthy middle, classes, so this in itself was a limitation on the sort of people who could benefit from such education, and even amongst that class, all were not educated. Outside the convent, opportunities for education would have been even slighter, even towards the end of the Middle Ages. In the early fifteenth century a French lay-woman, Christine de Pizan, can lament her own lack of education in youth. Neither of her parents believed in educating girls, though Christine was later to realize that this was 'more by custom than by right'. If things were done rightly, she believed boys and girls should be properly educated. At least she learnt to read and write, and thus armed was able to undo the damage wrought in youth. In later life, a widow and already making a name as a poetess, she embarked on a reading programme which enabled her to move away from what she considered to be the wretchedness of ignorance. She was lucky in that the position her family had enjoyed whilst her father was patronized by Charles V of France had given her friends useful to bookish pursuits. Gilles Malet, librarian of the king's library, was a friend, as were royal officials such as Guillaume de Tignonville, Bureau de la Rivière and Jean de Montagu. Jean Gerson, who was to defend her point of view in a celebrated literary quarrel, was chancellor of Paris university. Christine's great patron Louis of Orléans was building up a library to which she may have had access (McLeod, 1976, pp. 77–8). At any rate, she became acquainted with world history and some philosophy, but especially with poetry. Certainly she read Virgil, Ovid and Horace – probably in translation – and Dante who would have been accessible to her because she herself was Italian by birth. She obviously drank in much French poetry, though she has mainly critical censure for Jean de Meun's *Roman de la Rose*. Her contemporary, Eustache Deschamps, met with her admiration. The success of her educational programme shows itself in the vast quantity of her written works, to be dealt with a little later. But such education as Christine had in youth was given at home.

Christine's own daughter took the veil at the abbey of Poissy, and towards the end of her days Christine retired to an abbey – very possibly Poissy – though probably not as a professed nun (see McLeod, 1976, p. 159). Not all those women who lived in nunneries had taken permanent vows, so the word 'nun' does not always mean one thing. Probably from the Carolingian period onwards the word 'canoness' was used to indicate a woman who resided in a convent without a permanent vow. Such women took vows of chastity and obedience but not poverty, and so they could have servants and retain property such as books. Christine de Pizan in one of her early works, *Le Livre du Dit de Poissy* (c.1400), tells of a springtime visit to her daughter's abbey where the actual meal and entertainment took place not with the nuns, such as her daughter, but with the ladies, whose dress and way of life was considerably less austere than those of the nuns proper (Pizan, *Oeuvres Poétiques*, II, 159–222). Most of the women who lived a monastic life, with or without vows, received some education. They were taught religious studies above all, but also crafts such as spinning, weaving and embroidery. Many nuns also probably developed and passed on medical and nursing skills to their pupils. Hildegard of Bingen, one of the great female figures of the Church in her day (1098–1178), and best known for her religious writings, wrote two books on medicine, one of which was called *Physica*. It dealt with the nature of man and of the various elements, and about various creatures and plants and the ways in which they can be useful to man. Her book is full of descriptions, advice and superstitions. The cures she suggests – the use of dead frogs for gout and suchlike – are presumably part superstition, part experience, and much of it is very sound homely wisdom. It is possible that the association of monasteries, and more especially certain of their inmates, with powers of healing is based on the fund of medical and nursing lore acquired over many decades, and passed from one generation of nuns to another. Incidentally, monasteries tended to be well positioned, with a good water supply and a healthy diet which would have made them valuable as places of healing (Eckenstein, p. 270).

It is probable that more women learned to read than could actually write. The two skills by no means went together, and evidence of the possession of books does not necessarily indicate that their owners could also write. Wormald draws attention to the fact that the only two secular (as distinct from clerical) wills dating from the Anglo-Saxon period which mention books are those of women. Surviving wills of laymen make no mention of books (Wormald, p. 110). Criseyde in Chaucer's *Troilus and Criseyde* certainly possessed a literate female attendant, who could read to her mistress and her companions. When Pandarus comes looking for his niece at the beginning of Book II he finds her sitting with two other ladies

> withinne a paved parlour, and they thre
> Herden a mayden reden hem the geste
> Of the siege of Thebes, while hem leste. (II, 82–4)

(within a paved parlour, and the three of them heard a maiden read to them the geste of the siege of Thebes, while it pleased them.)

Writing was a different matter. Not all the women who could read and had access to works of literature, piety and scholarship, could also write. Such an additional qualification could be a matter of comment. One of the many attractions of Héloise for the philosopher Abelard was, on his own admission in the *Historia Calamitatum*, her knowledge and love of letters, so that 'even when separated we could enjoy each other's presence by exchange of written messages, in which we could speak more openly than in person, and so need never lack the pleasures of conversation' (Abelard and Héloise, p. 66). For Abelard, Héloise was clearly exceptional in all respects. Her keen intellect as well as her powerful emotional being are revealed in her own letters. She was gifted enough to appreciate his intellectual powers, woman enough to respond to his physical attractions:

> For your manhood was adorned by every grace of mind and body, and among the women who envied me then, could there be one now

who does not feel compelled by my misfortune to sympathize with my loss of such joys? (Abelard and Héloise, p. 115)

In their final separation, he to monastic vows, she to a convent, her command of words allows her to beg most movingly for at least a letter from him to compensate for his absence and her deprivation:

> I beg you then to listen to what I ask – you will see that it is a small favour which you can easily grant. While I am denied your presence, give me at least through your words – of which you have enough and to spare – some sweet semblance of yourself. (Abelard and Héloise, p. 116)

Letters were probably their only means of contact, and her obvious consolation, for the rest of their lives. Héloise was exceptional in her learning. Her learning was known in Paris before she knew Abelard. Even in her subsequent seclusion she was revered by layman and cleric alike for scholarship and wisdom. Abelard in a letter to Héloise's nuns of the Paraclete congratulates them on having in her a mother who is

> not unfamiliar not only with Latin but also with Greek and Hebrew literature, and appears to be the only woman now living who has attained that knowledge of the three languages which is extolled above all things by St Jerome as a matchless grace. (Epist. IX, PL CLXXVIII, trans. McLeod, 1938, p. 182)

Knowledge of Latin was necessary for any medieval scholar, but knowledge of Greek and Hebrew would have been a rare accomplishment for anyone, man or woman, in the twelfth century. Her praises were also sung by Peter and Venerable (Pernoud, pp. 54ff.).

At the other end of the scale, only one of the Paston women, whose letters survive from the fifteenth century, gives any evidence that she could write, and then only her name. Three of Margery Paston's letters – the texts of which are in different hands – appear to be signed by herself:

> Be youre servaunt (and bedewoman)
> Margery Paston.

The signatures are written in what Davis calls 'the same distinctively halting and uncontrolled hand, as of someone beginning to learn to write' (*The Paston Letters*, p. xxxvii). For the text of the letters themselves, she was dependent on amanuenses.

It is very likely that two of the most respected women mystical writers of the twelfth century, Elizabeth of Schönau and Hildegard of Bingen, did not actually write their own work. Hildegard was helped by two nuns, Richardis, sister of Hartwich, bishop of Bremen (1148–68), and Hiltrud of Sponheim. In fact, when Heinrich, archbishop of Mainz, advocated promoting Hiltrud to the rank of abbess in another convent, Hildegard, whose surviving correspondence is voluminous, wrote him an angry letter threatening him that 'your days are numbered, remember how Nebuchadnezzar fell and lost his crown' (Hildegard of Bingen, Epist. V). As a matter of interest, Heinrich was deposed soon afterwards and died in exile (Eckenstein, p. 272). Elizabeth was a nun of the convent attached to the Benedictine monastery of Schönau. She went there in 1141 and became lady superior in 1157. It is believed that her brother Ekbert, first a canon at Bonn and later a monk at Schönau, himself a writer of some importance, helped her to get her work into circulation. She was probably helped by fellow nuns to get it into written form. In an introduction to the *Visiones* of her first books, written by Ekbert after he had become abbot of Schönau (1167), he says that he collected these writings and other things that have reference to them, and has translated into Latin what was in German (Eckenstein, 278). She also wrote a *Liber Viarum Dei* (On the Ways of God), the title at any rate possibly in imitation of the *Scivias* of Hildegard, whose work she was acquainted with, and a *Liber Revelationum De Sacro Exercitu Virginum Coloniensium* (Revelations on the Holy Band of Virgins of Cologne). These two women were most highly regarded in their own day, and the fact that they did not actually write down their own work in no way detracts from their creative endeavour. Indeed, the great Italian mystic,

Catherine of Siena (1347–80), dictated the *Letters* and *Dialogues* which caused her to be one of only two women honoured with the title Doctor of the Church.

In fifteenth-century England, Margery Kempe, wife of a burgess of Lynn in Norfolk and mother of fourteen children, achieved great fame, not to say notoriety, by her visions and public 'cries'. She wrote her *Book of Margery Kempe* with the aid of amanuenses. Her lack of writing ability likewise did not diminish her influence, as she was regarded by many as a woman of great spirituality, and her mystical experiences are revealed in this autobiography. Her denunciation of all pleasure led to accusations of Lollardy, but on the whole she had many supporters, especially amongst the friars, both Dominicans and Carmelites. However, her habit of crying in church upset one celebrated preaching friar at Lynn who was not inclined to accept her distress as a mark of the success of his sermon. She had been so moved by his words on the Passion of our Lord that she burst out crying 'and cryid wonder sore . . .' (Kempe, p. 224). The friar was not amused and ruled, in spite of much intercession from her friends, that she be excluded from his sermons, 'and that was, to her, great pain'. However, other preachers were more tolerant, knowing that the sermon was 'to her the highest comfort on earth' (Kempe, pp. 227–8). This housewife and mother who subsequently took vows of chastity with her husband before Philip Repingdon, bishop of Lincoln (1413), seems to have enjoyed a sense of closeness to Jesus Christ and been favoured with signs of His love, and was sufficiently important to have her story written down.

Women writers on both religious and other subjects, however, did tend to be found in convents, and one of the most remarkable, as well as one of the earliest is Hrotswitha, a canoness of the Benedictine monastery of Gandersheim in Saxony. She is the earliest poet known in Germany and, by virtue of her six plays, is the first known dramatist of Western Europe after the fall of the ancient Roman stage. Both her date of birth and date of death are uncertain, but she probably lived c.935–1001/2, and what is known of her has to be gleaned from her own work and from contemporary annals. Gandersheim was one of the first religious houses to be founded in Saxony after the acceptance there of Christianity. Hrotswitha herself recorded its history in the *Primordia Cenobii Gandersheimensis*. It had been founded by Duke Liudolf at the request of his Frankish wife Oda and her mother Aeda, and the first three abbesses were daughters of Liudolf and Oda, grandparents of Henry the Fowler. It thus fell into the mould of other early religious foundations mentioned in Chapter 2, founded, patronized and ruled by members of a royal house. The Carolingian renaissance made Germany, especially Saxony, a place of learning, and with such great patronage Gandersheim became very rich and distinguished. Learning and literary activity surrounded Hrotswitha: Scholars, churchmen and royalty came and went, and her friend and teacher was the abbess Gerberga II, a granddaughter of Henry the Fowler who was crowned Holy Roman Emperor in 962. Liudolf and Oda, the founders of Gandersheim, had acquired sacred relics at Rome of Popes Anastasius and Innocent, and they became Gandersheim's patron saints. Hrotswitha wrote her *Vita Paparum* about them. The *Carmen De Gestis Oddonis* she wrote in praise of Otto I, uncle of Abbess Gerberga, a patron of learning and benefactor of the Church. It was a history of his reign. Hrotswitha entered the convent during his reign, possibly in 955, and as a young girl had many years of teaching and training. Her knowledge of classical and Christian literature indicates the library facilities which were available to her at Gandersheim. She admits that Terence's comedies influenced her plays, and she probably was acquainted with Virgil's *Aeneid*, possibly the *Georgics* and *Eclogues* and Ovid's *Metamorphoses*. It is likely that she also read early Christian authors such as Prudentius and Venantius Fortunatus, as well as Boethius. It is believed that she had some knowledge of philosophy, mathematics, astronomy and music. Her poetry is written in heroic classical metres, dactylic hexameters or in the elegiac verse composed of two-lined strophes, alternately dactylic hexameter and pentameter. Though her models were classical, she used a rhymed modification which was popular amongst early medieval writers.

Her first writings were eight legends in verse, based on apocryphal gospels and saints' legends which seem to have inspired her particularly. The first, *Maria*, is in honour of the Blessed Virgin and is based on the apocryphal gospel of St James. The third is of Gongolf, a Frankish leader of the Merovingian age; beautiful and godly, he was betrayed and murdered by his wife, who is subsequently punished. The fourth is the story of Pelagius, a Spanish youth who fell victim to a lecherous moorish tyrant. She says she heard the story from a visitor from Cordova, who had been an eye-witness. So her material is varied and drawn from far and wide. The first five legends are prefaced to Abbess Gerberga II, the last three have an additional dedication (see Hrotswitha, pp. xxvi–xxxvi). She describes herself as young in years, not much advanced in learning. She is writing in secret for fear those more learned than herself would put a stop to her work, on account of what she calls its crudeness. The agonies of the budding writer and scholar are amply portrayed. She offers her little volume for criticism, in the hope of being corrected, not ridiculed. She apologizes for the faultiness of some of her sources. She had not been aware when she started that authenticity of some of her material was questionable. She worked alone, in secret, often destroying what she did not like. She works to improve her talent and ability, lest neglect would cause it to rust, and labours for the greater glory of God. Her gratitude to her teachers is marked; she mentions one Rikkardis, and her special dedication is to her abbess, 'Royal Gerberga', who is her junior in years but her senior in wisdom and learning 'as befits a niece of the emperor'. She hopes her work will enhance the praise of her abbess and teacher. The legends and her historical and biographical writings would have seemed a large enough canon of works for a tenth-century nun, but in fact she is best known for yet another literary undertaking: her six rhymed dramas, the most original contribution to literature at that period. As her experience of writing grew, so did her confidence and she was better able to explain her purposes in the prefaces to the plays. The six plays, *Gallicanus*, *Dulcitius*, *Calimachus*, *Abraham*, *Paphnutius*, and *Sapientia* were modelled in structure on the plays of Terence, and she also shows the influence of the mimistic tradition and of the liturgy. Haight lists thirty-eight known performances of her plays from 1888 to 1963. Clearly they have been felt to be theatrically practical, in spite of the lack of general knowledge of drama in Western Europe from the fall of Rome until the development of liturgical drama and then the miracle and morality plays in the later Middle Ages. Her indebtedness to Terence is acknowledged in the preface to her plays. Her fascination for his charm of manner had overcome the fear of being corrupted by the wickedness of his matter. Her second preface is to 'Certain Learned Patrons of this Book'. Whatever Hrotswitha's modesty in regard to her work, Abbess Gerberga took pride in her pupil, and brought her work to the attention of scholarly visitors to Gandersheim, especially William of Mainz, illegitimate son of Otto I, and the king, Otto II. Hrotswitha submitted her *Gesta Oddonis* both to Gerberga and to Archbishop William for appraisal. The six plays, added to her other poetical, historical and biographical works, make Hrotswitha a most remarkably prolific, wide ranging authoress by the standards of any century, and in her own time she stands alone.

Hrotswitha was fortunate to live in a place where learning was pursued and among people who valued scholarship. In later centuries other German convents produced works and writers which could in turn lay claim to fame. The convent at Hohenburg in Alsace in the twelfth century housed the Abbess Herrad who compiled the *Hortus Deliciarum*, or Garden of Delights, a great encyclopedia decorated with beautiful illuminations, embodying the knowledge of the age. This magnificent illuminated manuscript, a fund of information on the knowledge, manners, customs and whole way of life in the twelfth century, was destroyed in 1870 when Strasbourg was bombarded by the Germans. A complete copy of the text was also lost.

The community of Helfta, founded in 1229 by Burkhardt, count of Mansfeld, for his daughters and other women of the Thuringian nobility, shows forth a whole crop of women writers, who produced their mystical writings for women. The annals of the house mention Elizabeth and Sophie, daughters of Hermann von Mansfeld. Elizabeth was a good painter and Sophie a scribe of numerous books (Eckenstein, p. 329). This confirms the possibility that nuns did write well enough to produce manuscripts, even such a one as the Munich manuscript of Hrotswitha's works. Sophie was prioress before Gertrud, whose incumbency from 1251–91 marks the climax of the house's prosperity. Gertrud established the house as a centre of culture and learning, encouraging the collecting of books and the transcribing of them by her nuns. She caused the nuns to be taught the liberal arts. Latin was taught and written by the nuns. Three women, especially, made the house famous: Mechthild of Magdeburg, Mechthild von Hackeborn (Abbess Gertrud's sister) educated at Helfta, and Gertrud the Great, not to be confused with the abbess of the same name.

Mechthild of Magdeburg lived in a Béguine house there, 1235–68. Béguines were associated with Lambert Le Bégue (stammerer) of Liège (d. 1177). The Béguinages are associated mainly with the Netherlands but did spread to some French and German towns. They were very popular amongst women of all classes and had mainly philanthropic aims, caring for the sick and needy. They did not have vows and were free to leave the community and marry. Such freedoms often brought them severe censure, as happened to orders such as that of Fontevrault. Such a mixed group of women could incline to a variety of paths, to mysticism or to heresy, sometimes to vagrancy. Mechthild began her mystical work while still at Magdeburg. Her writings were collected by her friends and distributed under the title *Das Fliessende Licht der Gottheit* (The Flowing

Light of the Godhead). These seven books or divisions of prayers, meditations, visions and reflections on the times were written in German, and about 1290 six books were translated into Latin as *Revelationes*. The seventh book was written at Helfta, to which she came in 1268, as her criticisms of the local clergy at Magdeburg had made her quite unpopular.

Mechthild von Hackeborn was known and loved by her fellow nuns for her tenderness and religious fervour; as well as being a musician she wrote a *Liber Specialis Gratiae*, the name of which was given to her by a heavenly voice. Translated into English in the fifteenth century as *The Book of Gostlye Grace*, it is composed of five parts: Part I has references to festal days of the Church, to Christ, Mary and the Saints; Part II speaks of manifestations of Divine Grace in Mechthild herself; Parts III and IV tell how God should be praised and how we should be saved; in Part V she converses with people who are dead, especially members of the convent; Parts VI and VII were added after Mechthild's death by other nuns, and contain information about her sister, Abbess Gertrud, details about Mechthild's death, and visions other nuns have had of her (Eckenstein, pp. 345–6).

Gertrud the Great came to Helfta in 1261 as a child, and may well have been of lowly origin. Her studies were grounded in the liberal arts, and she was greatly influenced by the sisters Abbess Gertrud and Mechthild of Hackeborn. She was able to translate from Latin into German. She is reputed to have made many books of extracts and collections of passages from the Church Fathers. A vision at the age of twenty-five caused her to devote herself entirely to religious study. Information about her is to be gleaned from the first part of her *Legatus Divinae Pietatis* (Legacy of Divine Piety), one of the finest literary products of Christian mysticism. Only the second book was actually written by her, the other four were based on her notes. In Book II she writes of how she realized an approximation to things divine, such as reverence, love and the desire for knowledge alone can secure. She can speak of how God didst inspire me with the thought that if, conscious of thy grace, I flow back to be joined to thee like water; if, growing in the knowledge of virtue like unto these trees, I flower in the greenness of good deeds; if, looking down on things earthly in free flight like these doves, I approach heaven, and with my bodily senses removed from external turmoil, apprehend thee with my whole mind, then in joyfulness my heart will make for thee a habitation. (Eckenstein, pp. 348–9)

She said she wrote her *Legacy* 'to the increase of God's power' and out of 'obedience to thy will, desire for thy glory, and zeal for the salvation of souls'. The subsequent history of the work must bear out her success in these aims, for it was repeatedly printed in Latin, sometimes with the *Liber Specialis Gratiae* of Mechthild of Hackeborn. It was translated into German and English. She also wrote a collection of prayers, *Exercita Spiritualia* (Spiritual Exercises) which gained great popularity. Though she has never been canonized, her cult was first authorized in 1606 and extended to the whole Catholic Church by Clement XIII in 1738. She has been included in the Roman martyrology since 1677. These three women produced mystical works which were both significant in their own time and of lasting influence.

One of the small group of recognized English mystics in the later Middle Ages is another woman, Julian of Norwich. Margery Kempe, already mentioned, though her work is of a rather different character, is probably to be associated with them (see Knowles, p. 120, n. 3). Little is known about Julian, but she probably lived rather a different life from the nuns at Helfta. She seems to have been an anchoress, living a solitary life of silence, prayer and mortification outside the walls of St Julian's church, Norwich. Her *Sixteen Revelations of Divine Love* were written down some twenty years after the experience which provoked them – a series of fifteen revelations in a state of ecstasy lasting five hours on 8 May 1373, followed by one further vision the next day.

By English standards, Julian of Norwich and Margery

Kempe are exceptional ladies, exceptional in their mystical powers, and in the power of expression which caused their experiences to be recorded. They are exceptional by the standards of the German writers just mentioned in that they had no close association with a religious community or convent, Margery, indeed, being a lay-woman.

The English nun in the later Middle Ages is a poor descendant indeed of her pious, disciplined and scholarly ancestors of Anglo-Saxon times. Two things in the main were probably responsible for this deterioration. The doubtful piety of those forced vocations mentioned in the previous chapter would have had a deleterious effect on the spiritual life of nunneries in the later Middle Ages, and the redoubled efforts to enforce enclosure upon nuns in order to safeguard a correct pattern of moral behaviour had the added effect of cutting them off from the best male teachers of the day. This in turn meant that the standard of tuition which could be offered to girls in a convent was not high. The universities, once founded, ignored the existence of women as being able to acquire knowledge, and so appropriated only to men the privileges of a university education. Indeed, the pursuit of knowledge itself seemed to be regarded as a thoroughly masculine activity. Nevertheless, a convent education still seems to have conferred a certain status, even on those who subsequently returned to the world. Chaucer's Reeve tells in his Tale of the Miller's wife who was *come of noble kyn; she was ifostryd in a nonnerye*, and on account of her kindred and the *nortelry* (education) she had learned, no one dared call her anything but 'Madame'. In the nunneries devotional interest, including books relating to such devotions, were cultivated to the exclusion of everything else. The decline in general scholastic attainments can be charted. In the twelfth century Queen Maud (or Matilda), daughter of Margaret of Scotland and wife of Henry I, was able to write fluent Latin and make references to the scriptures and the Church Fathers, as well as to Pythagoras and Socrates. She was the product of a convent education at Romsey, and only 'came out' when declared free to marry by Anselm. There is extant a twelfth-century *Life of St Catherine* in Norman French by Sister Clemence, a nun at Barking. In the opening lines she says that she translated it from Latin into French (Paris, pp. 400–3).

> Je ki la vie ai translatee
> Par nun sui Clemence numee,
> Qe Berekinge sui nunain.

(I who have translated the Life am called Clemence by name, I am a nun of Barking.)

The early-thirteenth-century *Ancrene Riwle* gives evidence that the sisters for whom it was intended knew Latin and French as well as English. However, though Latin continued to be studied in all convents down to the Reformation, it was not pursued to the same extent as in earlier centuries. In the south of England especially, French gradually took its place. For instance, in 1310 the bishop of Winchester drew up a list of injunctions for the convent at Romsey as a result of a visit. A literal translation into French was appended to it for the nuns' convenience. Examples can be found in the fourteenth century where French alone is used in communications to nuns from bishops or other churchmen without any Latin being used. From the Norman Conquest to the middle of the fourteenth century, French was the language of the upper classes as well as the language of the Law, and French was the language of literary and devotional works also. Letters written by nuns at this period tend to be in French, by comparison with Hildegard of Bingen's voluminous Latin correspondence in twelfth-century Germany. By the fifteenth century Latin and French had both been abandoned for English in the nunneries (see Power, 1922, pp. 246–7). A rhymed version of the Rule of St Benedict was written for nuns in English in a northern dialect between 1400 and 1425 (Böddekker, pp. 60–93). In the preface the translator gives his reason for making the translation:

> Monkes and als all leryd men
> In latyn may it lyghtly ken,

And wytt þarby how þay sall wyrk
To sarue god and haly kyrk;
Bott tyll women to mak it couth,
Þat leris no latyn in þar ȝouth,
In ingles is it ordand here,
So þat þay may it lyghtly lere. (9–16)

(Monks and learned men also may know it [the Rule] in Latin, and know easily how they must work to serve God and Holy Church; but it is arranged here into English in order to make it known to women who learn no Latin in their youth, so that they may easily learn it.)

Later in the fifteenth century the Register of Godstow, a wealthy Benedictine nunnery, was prepared in English under the rule of Abbess Alice Henly. It included an A.B.C. of devotion and an English translation of all the charters of the house. Some could be found who had criticized the availability of devotional and spiritual material in English precisely *because* it made them more available to women, as did the chronicler Knighton, who bewailed the availability of even so basic a book as the Bible, as translated by Wycliffe:

> Transtulit de Latino in Anglicam linguam non angelicam . . . unde per ipsum fit vulgare et magis apertum laicis, et mulieribus legere scientibus, quam solet esse clericis admodum literatis et bene intelligentibus, et sic evangelica margarita spargitur et a porcis conculcatur. (Knighton, II, 151–2)

(he [Wycliffe] has translated [the Gospel] into the English (not angelic) tongue . . . whence through that very man it becomes common and more open to laymen and to women who know how to read than it is wont to be to very literate clergymen of good understanding, and the pearl of the gospel is scattered and trampled by swine.)

But the compiler of the Godstow register wished women of religion to be excused from understanding much of the content of Latin works, and for fear of any harm coming to such women through misinformation or misunderstanding of Latin, he thought it necessary that they should have works written in their mother tongue. He also describes the inmates of Godstow as 'for the most part well learned in English Books' (Eckenstein, p. 360).

Prospects, then, for educating women even for the religious life seem to have deteriorated in the later Middle Ages. Those women whose work has survived, like Julian of Norwich and Margery Kempe, are exceptions. Chaucer's Prioress, believed to be a 'type' like all his other pilgrims, probably gives a more reliable witness to the average woman of religion in the fourteenth century. She speaks French, but French

> After the Scole of Stratford Atte Bowe
> For French of Paris was to her unknowe. (*Gen. Prologue*, 125–6)

The Norman French of the conquerors had once linked the new English aristocracy with its French ancestors and relatives, but with the passage of time it became as much a divider of the two nations as the English language itself, by virtue of the differences between Anglo-Norman and continental French. It is possible, therefore, that Chaucer is merely telling us that the Prioress spoke bad French. The Lady Prioress, called 'Madame' as befitted one educated in a nunnery and consecrated to Jesus Christ, is presented with the satirist's touch, and the fact that she does not appear as either particularly scholarly or particularly pious is, no doubt, a reflection of current trends. She does not appear to have the complete collection of faults levelled at nuns by many medieval satirists. It is never stated in so many words that she is sensual, quarrelsome, deceitful, luxurious, indiscreet, lacrimose and hungry for praise, faults indeed common to all women in the eyes of the satirist (see Mann, p. 129). Some of the waywardness is gently suggested, however. Her partiality for fine clothes and for ornament links her with ladies whose secular status might have rendered such a weakness less heinous.

> Ful semyly hir wympul pynched was . . .
> Ful fetys was hir cloke, as I was war.

Of smal coral, aboute hire arm she bar
A peire of bedes, gauded al with grene,
And thereon heng a brooch of gold ful sheene.
(*Gen. Prologue*, 150–60)

(Her wimple was closely pleated very becomingly . . . her cloak was very well made, as I was aware. Around her arm she carried rosary beads of small coral, adorned at intervals with green beads, and thereon hung a brooch of very bright gold.)

The beautiful beads are at least a religious emblem, but the brooch would appear to be a vain adornment. Whether the motif on the brooch itself –

On which there was first write a crowned A
And after *Amor Vincit omnia*

hints at a desire for sensual pursuits or whether it reminds us of the spiritual love which should and does conquer all is a matter for perennial debate. The pursuit of God's love was appropriate to a nun, the pursuit of sensual love all too common among fourteenth-century nuns. Her delightful table manners, such that

She leet no morsel from her lippes falle
Ne wette hir fyngres in hir sauce depe,
(*Gen. Prologue*, 128–9)

have as a literary model those advocated by the Duenna in the *Roman de la Rose* as a means of attracting the opposite sex. Thus the hint of interests outside those of the spiritual life is lodged quite early in her 'portrait'.

Her female tearfulness which might have been directed more appropriately towards weeping for the sins of mankind (Mann, p. 129, n. 16) is spent in crying for mice caught in traps or for her little dogs (*Gen. Prologue*, 144 and 148–9). The overall impression created by this nun is of a fine lady, 'Madame Eglantyne', who is *symple and coy*, and who only swears by St Loy (*Gen. Prologue*, 119–20).

Her lack of scholarship is not a matter for overt comment as it is in the case of Chaucer's Monk:

> What sholde he studie and make hymselven wood [mad]
> Upon a book in cloystre alwey to poure.
> *(Gen. Prologue,* 184–5)

Nor is there any reference to the fact that she is out of her convent, whereas had she heeded the injunctions of contemporary bishops she would certainly not have been on pilgrimage at all (*Gen. Prologue,* ed. Hodgson, p. 81). It is the Monk also who elicits the direct comment that a monk out of his cloister is *likened til a fissh that is waterlees* (*Gen. Prologue,* 180). The Prioress is presented with all the naive enthusiasm of Chaucer the Pilgrim (Donaldson, pp. 3ff.), who makes no overt criticism, but who highlights her appearance, *Hir mouth ful smal, and therto softe and reed* (*Gen. Prologue,* 153), her dress, her manners, her 'elegant' French and her compassion for the pet dogs she should never have owned. There is only the merest hint, in the title of her office, her beads and her singing of the Divine Office, that she is bound to a cloistered spirituality. There is no suggestion whatever that she might have been a scholar. The narrator's final couplet on the subject of the Prioress' companions does nothing to improve this impression:

> Another Nonne with hire hadde she
> That was hir chapeleyne, and preestes thre.
> *(Gen. Prologue,* 163–4)

Another nun would have been an invaluable companion to her as a chaperone, in order to preserve the proprieties; but the word *chapeleyne* means 'secretary', a sort of administrative assistant, presumably as crucial in her way to the Lady Prioress as Hiltrud had been to Hildegard of Bingen. That three priests seem otiose for the prioress of so small a convent as St Leonard's Stratford-atte-Bowe was pointed out by Manly (p. 508), yet the *Preestes thre* occur in a line that is unusual in that it has no manuscript variations (Donaldson, p. 62). No Chaucerian scribe ever doubted that there were, or could have been, three priests attending the Prioress of this portrait. The make-up of her retinue reinforces the impression of the Prioress already lodged in her portrait;

> And sikerly, she was of great disport,
> And ful pleasaunt, and amyable of port,
> And peyned hire to countrefete cheere
> Of court, and to been estatlich of manere
> And to ben holden digne of reverence.
> (*Gen. Prologue*, 137–40)

(And surely, she was very entertaining and very pleasant and amiable of bearing, and took pains to imitate the behaviour of the court, and to be dignified of manner, and to be considered worthy of deep respect.)

She is so much a lady that a secretary to look after her tedious business affairs could scarcely be done without, and so attractive a woman that not one but three men, albeit priests, dance in attendance.

10

The Literate Lay-Woman

What then, of the women who remained in the world and their contributions to literature? As always we can speak only of the aristocrats or those brought up in court circles. Not many such women are well known as writers, but what they lack in performance they seem to have made up for in patronage of literature and the arts. An example is provided as early as the ninth century of a lay-woman venturing to write. Dhuoda, a Carolingian noblewoman, wife of Bernard de Septimanie, wrote a *Liber Manualis* (c.841–3) for her son Guillaume. He was aged sixteen and was entering into the service of Charles the Bald. A manual was a handbook, to be used daily, a little work of spirituality or morals. She writes to Guillaume: 'Tu y trouveras aussi un miroir dans lequel tu pourras contempler sans hésitation le salut de ton âme' (Dhuoda, p. 81). Dhuoda was an aristocrat, educated according to her station. She refers to books she used in making her Manual, without always giving their titles. This indicates that she made the book herself, and did not order anyone else such as a chaplain to do it (Dhuoda, Introd. pp. 32–3). She seems to have been quite well read in pre-Carolingian literature, though she mentions only one name, Donat, and two works, the *Synonyms* of Isidore of Seville, and the *Regula Pastoralis* of Gregory the Great. She appreciated poetry and cites the *Cathemerinon* of Prudentius. She also appears to have been acquainted with the work of St Augustine. She knew the Bible and often quotes from it, especially the Old Testament – the Sapiential Books, Job, and the Psalter. Of the New Testament, she quotes St Matthew. In addition, she must have read hagiographical and moral works, and devotions for private prayer. The *Liber Manualis* treats of vices and virtues, but also seeks to remind her son about his God, and his ancestors. Dhuoda tells him of his duty to his father and to his overlord the king. She tells him the way to perfection, by way of a comparison between the seven gifts of the Holy Spirit and the eight beatitudes – fifteen steps by which he can climb towards perfection. Altogether, Dhuoda's Manual for her son has left us with some idea of the intellectual and cultural life of a ninth-century Western European lay noblewoman, as well as bearing witness to her own moral and intellectual worth. It is sad to conclude that, good as Dhuoda's advice was, her family lived in troubled times, and six years after she had poured her heart out to her son in this moving work, Guillaume was beheaded for treason.

Only two other women are featured in this chapter, the one a twelfth-century poetess calling herself 'of France', and about whose personal life very little is known, the other Italian by birth, French by upbringing, whose life and work take us through the end of the fourteenth century and into the fifteenth. Marie de France is the earliest known French poetess. As well as writing twelve *Lais*, she also composed a collection of *Fables* and an *Espurgatoire S. Patrice*. In the Epilogue to the *Fables* she tells us her name: *Marie ai nun, Si sui de France*. In the opening lines of the *Lai of Guigemar* she also calls herself Marie. Of the *Fables*, she herself tells us that she is translating them from English into French at the request of one Count William – *Pur amur le Cunte Williame, Le plus vaillant de nul realme* (For the love of Count William, the most worthy of any kingdom). In lines 30–2 of the Prologue she had described him as *flurs de chevalerie, d'enseignement, de curteisie* (flower of knightly virtues, of wisdom and of courtly behaviour). 'Translate' need not be taken literally; it may mean simply to compose in French on the basis of an English original. From this information it is usually reckoned that she was of French origin, but living in England, knowing English and working for an English patron. The *Lais* she wrote for a king, as she tells us in the Prologue:

En l'honur de vus, nobles reis,
Ki tant estes pruz e curteis (43–4)

(In honour of you, noble king who are so valliant and courteous.)

Whether this king was Henry II or his young son Henry 'au cort mantel', styled king from 1170 to 1183, or even King John is a matter of some dispute.

Marie knew Latin as well as English, for in the Prologue to the *Lais* she tells us that she had considered – and rejected – the idea of translating some *bone estoire* from Latin into French in favour of composing the *Lais*. The *Espurgatoire S. Patrice* is based on a Latin original. She says (Marie de France, *Espurgatoire*, 2297–300) that she 'put it into *Romanz*'. She wrote in the last third of the twelfth century, probably c.1160–80, and it may be that this shadowy figure was not a lay-woman at all, but the natural daughter of Godefroy d'Anjou (father of Henry II) who became abbess of Shaftesbury c.1181 (see Fox, pp. 303ff. and 317ff.).

However, there is also the possibility that she was the daughter of Count Waleran de Neular, and wife of Hue Talbot who lived in Herefordshire and Devon (see Holmes, p. 189). The only complete manuscript of the *Lais* is BL Harley 978, and it is also the oldest. It is Anglo-Norman, and it is very likely that she had patrons and was popular on both sides of the channel. In England, so-called 'Breton Lays' after the style of Marie de France were composed in English in the late thirteenth and in the fourteenth century. Even Chaucer was not immune from such influence for he allowed his Franklin to tell his fellow pilgrims that his Tale would be a Breton Lay. It is the *Lais* which have been responsible for her lasting fame, a fame which she seems to have acquired in her own time, if the testimony of her contemporary Denis Piramus in his *Vie Seint Edmund le Rei* is to be believed. According to him one Dame Marie wrote *Lais* for which she was 'much praised and the verses loved by all' (Denis Piramus, 39–40).

Of her twelve *Lais*, six are set on the continent, five in Britain, one other left rather vague. Six have proper names as titles, five of the others have titles referring to characters in the story. *Chevrefoil* is one of the few *Lais* whose title does not refer to a person or persons, and she translates this into English at the end as *Gotelef* (Goatleaf). She also translates the Breton title of *Laüstic* as *russignol* in French and *nihtegale* (nightingale) in English.

Some critics would argue that Marie was the first to write this kind of poem, which has been called a 'nouvelle en vers'. All other 'Breton Lays' (and there are anonymous *lais* of the Marie de France type) would thus be imitations. More cautious commentators draw attention to one or two similar narrative poems which were written before Marie's time and would argue that if she was not the first poet to write narrative *lais* inspired by certain musical compositions (also called *lais*) of Breton minstrels, then at least she was one of the first. She certainly raised the genre to the distinguished place it occupies in medieval literature. Making such poems with material of Celtic/British origin seems to have been Marie's own idea. Her *Lais* have been described as extolling the power and value of love (Stevens, p. 3). They have been said to indicate different kinds of love and to explore different aspects of the nature of love itself (Mickel, p. 41). Love in her *Lais* – and in others of the same kind which followed – generally leads to suffering, though it can have miraculous power over earthly suffering. It does not depend on marriage, and is often extra-marital, but it can also lead to marriage. Love can be selfish or generous, but in most cases it is immoderate. Happiness resides not in the self but in the happiness of the beloved. She presents love as powerful through time and through obstacles, as in *Milun* and *Guigemar*; it defies concealment in *Lanval*; it makes people attempt impossible things in *Les Deus Amanz*. It can be chaste, as in *Les Deus Amanz*, lustful as in *Equitan*, adulterous as in *Yonec* and *Chevrefoil*, charitable as in *Eliduc* or *Lai Le Fresne*. However, the great example of happy married love triumphing over suffering is not found in Marie's canon, but in the early thirteenth-century

Middle English 'Breton Lay' of *Sir Orfeo*, clearly modelled on her poems. The other two clear examples of Breton Lays in English, *Sir Launfal* and *Lay Le Frayn* are indications of her lasting popularity. *Lay Le Frayn*, surviving in an early thirteenth-century manuscript, and *Sir Launfal*, written by Thomas Chestre in the late fourteenth century (*Sir Launfal*, p. 15), are based on Marie's *Lai Le Fresne* and *Lanval*. There is also an early fourteenth-century English version of *Lanval* called *Landevale*.

It is to the late fourteenth century that we must turn to find a documented account of a woman writer, one of the most remarkable of the medieval period. Christine de Pizan was the daughter of an Italian astrologer, Tommaso de Benvenuto da Pizzano, invited to the court of France by Charles V when he came to the throne in 1364. Her father never went back to Italy, and after three or four years was joined in France by his wife and little daughter Cristina. They arrived in 1368. The king treated his 'Thomas de Pizan' well. He gave him 100 francs a month, and a fief of Orsonville in the commune of Villiers-en-Bière, south-east of Paris and east of Melun. Thomas also bought a castle, called Mémorant. Thus, Christine had a comfortable childhood, which was also very happy. Quite a lot of autobiographical details are found in two of her works, *La Mutacion de Fortune* and *Lavision*. In later life she was to regret her lack of formal education, and the fact that girls were not educated like boys. Her own respect for her father's learning was no doubt augmented by the fact that he was much valued by the king. Her mother whom she calls Dame Nature in the *Mutacion de Fortune* was her educator, forming her character and moral qualities, as well as the mental qualities necessary for dealing properly with life, giving her amongst other things discretion, consideration, retention and memory. Christine also believed herself endowed with eloquence and reason, though not with beauty (Pizan, *Mutacion de Fortune*, I, 25–33). In spite of this – even if what she says were true – she did not lack suitors. Many may have sought to advance themselves by marriage because of her father's position. Her father himself chose a graduate scholar Étienne de Castel as Christine's husband. He was not rich, though he came of a noble Picard family. He was, it appears, chosen for his character and virtue, though Christine speaks with admiration of the beauty of his face and body. The king showed his pleasure at the match by giving Étienne a vacant post as notary and secretary to himself. They married in 1379; she was fifteen and he was twenty-four. He promised to look after her, never desert her, and that they should be true friends. Christine praises him for his wisdom, courtesy and knowledge. He was loyal and loving, and considerate to the young girl in his care. The generosity of the king made them well off – as it had enriched her father. Their household was certainly comfortable. Christine bore children, a girl and a boy, and in between a boy who died.

Before the arrival of her children, the king died, and her father lost his great patron. Thomas became relatively poor, his income now dependent on irregular though handsome gifts. When Thomas died he left a widow and two sons, besides Christine. Étienne became head of the whole household. He had also found himself advisor to a young king half his age, Charles VI. For ten years Christine and Étienne lived happily. Christine adored her husband and he her. She was always to see a wife as neither a slave nor on a pedestal, but as a close friend of her husband – who nevertheless remained head of the house.

In 1389 when they had been married ten years, Étienne fell ill while accompanying the king to Beauvais. Among strangers and without a doctor in immediate attendance, he died. Christine was twenty-five, and utterly shattered by her loss. She became a recluse, 'dull, sad, alone and weary', as she tells in *Le Chemin de longue estude* (p. 6). In *La Mutacion de Fortune* (pp. 51–3) she tells how she longed for death, but fortune came and turned her into a man. She faced up to the responsibility of looking after herself and her children, as well as her mother and two brothers. She had to be tough, to fight for her rightful belongings. She had been in ignorance of Étienne's finances and it was thirteen or fourteen years before the estate was settled. She had to trail through different courts, begging people to plead for her, being accused of charming such male assistants for other reasons.

She had known King Charles VI and his brother Louis since childhood, and Louis was later to patronize her. She was also to be helped by Louis duke of Bourbon, the late queen's brother. However, she was very much alone at first in her struggle for financial independence. The court was in some disarray, as Charles VI became manic-depressive, needing a regent. Her friends encouraged her to write, for which she had already displayed some talent, and write she did. She commenced by writing twenty *Ballades* in which she seems to have purged her being of some of her grief and bitterness at the loss of her beloved Étienne. In the process she discovered a gift for writing skilful and beautiful love poems, and kept on writing till she had written 100 *Ballades*. As she went on she invented a love affair so convincing in its details and emotions that some of her friends really believed she had fallen in love again (Pizan, *Oeuvres Poétiques*, I, 1–20 and 21–100). She continued to write lyric verse at intervals in the course of her writing career, but of the various forms of lyric poetry open to her the only other one apart from the *Ballade* which she wrote successfully was the *Rondeau*. She wrote sixty-nine *Rondeaux*, the early ones also dealing with the loss of Étienne, which she can still scarcely bear, then turning to the theme of an imaginary lover (Pizan, *Oeuvres Poétiques*, I, 14–85).

Later *Ballades* leave the topic of love and treat of such things as morality and patriotism (Pizan, *Oeuvres Poétiques*, I, 209–79). She was not afraid to embark on longer works, and indeed her total output is staggering. Between 1397 and 1429 she wrote over twenty major works, not to mention hundreds of shorter poems, some of them occasional or dedicatory. The range of her work is also astonishing, both in prose and in poetry. Like Dhuoda she felt the need to commit advice to her son in writing. *Les Enseignements Moraux que je Christine donne à Jean de Castel mon fils* were probably produced in 1377 when the thirteen-year-old Jean left home to be trained in the noble household of the Earl of Salisbury (Pizan, *Oeuvres Poétiques*, III, 27–44). The *Épistre d'Othéa la déesse* in 1399 was also probably for Jean. With this book Christine began to tap the resource of princely patronage for the first time. She dedicated the first copy to Louis of Orleans, and would certainly have received the customary gift of money in return (McLeod, 1976, p. 52). Further copies she had made for the dukes of Burgundy and Berry, each with a dedicatory poem. She must have extended this useful method of publicity for herself and her poem as forty-eight other manuscripts survive, one of them very elaborately illustrated. In time she was to become too well known to need such publicity, but she continued to 'place' her work with great patrons.

Christine the moralist and the patriot was to emerge in prose works such as *La Prod'homie de l'homme* (unpublished, see McLeod, 1976, p. 178) mainly in praise of Louis of Orleans, and *Le Livre du Corps de Policie* on the 'body politic' of the nation, written with the dauphin in mind (McLeod, 1976, p. 123). With a horror for war and civil strife she penned *Le Livre des fais d'armes et de chevalrie* in the wake of the frightful murder of Louis of Orleans in 1407 (unpublished, see McLeod, 1976, p. 179). In 1410 she wrote *Lamentation sur les maux de la guerre civile* (see McLeod, 1976, p. 179) in the face of the growing threat of internal strife because of the duke of Burgundy's obvious intentions to rule France. Her last major work was *Le Livre de la Paix*, presented to the duke of Berry on 1 January 1414. Christine is a remarkable personality in two ways, first of all because of her driving ambition – which she fulfilled – to educate herself, and second for the defence of women to which she devoted not one but several of her works. Her self-imposed programme of educational reading, which she probably embarked on around 1400, resulted in a further stimulation of the creative impulse. Very early in this educational period she commenced *Le Livre de la Mutacion de Fortune*, an immense poem over 23,000 lines long, which opens with an account of her own life. The prose works *Le*

Chemin de longue estude and *Lavision* also show forth her greater learning, and her willingness to write on subjects other than love. The former contains moving details of her love for her dead husband. The latter she actually called *Lavision Christine*, thus underlining the personal details which lie behind the allegorical, dream-vision mould of the work.

Christine gave a copy of the *Mutacion de Fortune* to Philip of Burgundy as a New Year gift in 1404 – she also seems to have given a copy to the duke of Berry – and very shortly afterwards the duke honoured her by commissioning her to write an account of the life of his dead brother, Charles V. This was not to be an ordinary biography, but a record of Charles V's virtues and character. Such an invitation was a great honour for a woman writer, but Christine, whose family had received much largesse from the late king, was not an inappropriate choice. The resulting work was *Le Livre des fais et bonnes meurs de Charles V*, and it was completed in November 1404. It enhanced Christine's reputation in her own time and was long to be remembered after her death. It was also probably responsible for developing Christine's interest in political affairs, which remained for the rest of her life, and is obvious in many of her works.

Her championship of women emerged early in *L'Épistre au Dieu d'Amours* of 1399 (Pizan, *Oeuvres Poétiques*, II, 1–27). This was a venture into the attack on anti-feminist literature. Cupid, God of love, has received complaints from women of every rank, asking for help against the outrageous behaviour of disloyal men. Christine's central point is aimed at male writers who have taken such delight in belittling her sex. Her own scant education at this period does not allow her to refer to many such writers by name, but Ovid is criticized, as is Jean de Meun, thirteenth-century co-author of the *Roman de La Rose*. De Meun had devoted much space to the art of deceiving women. Christine goes on to defend women: there were some bad angels, are all angels bad? She refers to scripture: woman was not created of clay but of man, the most noble of creatures, and God chose to be born of woman. Women are not cruel, but kind. They do not maim and kill, or disinherit dependants, make false contracts or upset the kingdom. Cupid feels that woman's complaints, and all Christine's arguments, are so justified that he urges his court to punish those who have defamed women.

For a relatively unknown woman writer to criticize Jean de Meun was an extraordinarily bold action at a time when the greatness of the thirteenth-century poet was unquestioned and his work universally acclaimed. In 1401 she took up her pen to criticize him again, in reply to a letter (now lost) written to her by a friend, Jean de Montreuil, Provost of Lille. Montreuil had praised most highly the *Roman de la Rose*. Her long letter sparked off a literary quarrel known as the Debate on the *Roman de la Rose*. She accuses Jean de Meun of holding a cynical view of women, and, more seriously, of denigrating marriage, and promoting heterosexual promiscuity. For Christine, marriage was the ideal relationship between man and woman, and though not insensible to the many excellent qualities of the *Roman de la Rose* she is fearful that its very excellence will cause people to regard its views on women and its encouragements to vice too favourably. The arguments in her letter became widely known and caused some raised eyebrows in court and other circles. The king's secretary Gontier Col took up the cudgels on behalf of the *Roman de la Rose*, but his ill-mannered and threatening letter to Christine does him no credit. He begs for a copy of her original statement, and accuses her of being a mere mouthpiece for others too cowardly to speak, more than insinuating that a mere woman could not have thought up such arguments for herself. Following receipt of her original comments he launched into the attack again, reproving still more arrogantly her 'overweening presumption'.

Christine's reply to him is both courteous and daring. She repeats her criticisms of de Meun, and turns aside his criticisms of her feminine stupidity. Indeed she tells him not to keep his mind closed! She must have needed support from his malice however, as early in 1402 Christine sent copies of the correspondence to Queen Isabeau with a covering letter, and also to the Provost of Paris, Guillaume de Tignonville. Their replies, if any, do not survive, but Jean Gerson, Chancellor of the University of Paris and Canon of Notre Dame, showed himself a most powerful ally (McLeod, 1976, p. 69). In May 1402 he produced a long treatise criticizing the *Roman* for its bad influence on morals, indicating objections very close to those of Christine.

Gontier Col's brother Pierre took up the defence of the *Roman de la Rose* in a letter which he wrote in reply both to Christine and Gerson. Much of his venom is directed towards Christine and he is even more condescending and abusive than his brother. He compares her to the crow who, on being praised for its song, sang even louder and dropped its mouthful (McLeod, 1976, p. 70). It says much for Christine's sense of justice and courtesy that she actually took the trouble to reply to such a tirade. She resists the urge to take up each point he makes, speaks generally, and says that as each has his own view and neither can make the other change it, they must continue to differ. She admits that his sillier statements made her laugh. She signs herself 'Your well-wishing lover of learning, Christine'.

Only a fragment of a further letter from him remains, and there the debate seemed to rest. However, Christine's championship of women found other expressions, even while the debate raged. The *Dit de la Rose* (Pizan, *Oeuvres Poétiques*, II, 29–48) purports to describe an occasion on St Valentine's day, 1402, in a palace belonging to Louis of Orleans. She herself is present at a supper during which a lady called Loyalty magically appears. She is accompanied by young girls carrying gilded cups, and brings greetings from the God of Love. She also brings red roses on condition that the company present swear never to vilify women. She brings too the text of an oath which everyone who takes a rose must swear to keep, and guard the honour of women in all things. In this way, those present join the Order of the Rose. Christine expounds the meaning of all this in a dream she purports to have dreamt that same night after the company had broken up. Loyalty comes to her in her dream and explains why the God of Love sent her to institute the new order. The God of Love hates those who belittle or speak ill of women. The new order may only be conferred by women. Loyalty gives Christine a beautiful gold parchment containing the rules of the order, and empowers her to make them known everywhere. Thus in poetry Christine justifies her abiding interest in women's status in society.

La Cité des Dames is possibly the work for which she is most remembered, together with its sequel, *Le Livre de Trois Vertus*, which is called in some manuscripts *Le Trésor de la Cité des Dames* (both works unpublished, see McLeod, 1976, p. 178). In *La Cité des Dames* Christine is invited to build an ideal city for all ladies of good repute by three sisters who are called Reason, Rectitude and Justice. While the building is in progress, Christine converses with the ladies who tell her much about the place of women in history, illustrated by references to such women as Lucrece, Penelope and Dido. Reason explains that men have vilified women on two accounts – one, because of Eve, and two, because men suspect women of being their superiors, but wish it to be kept quiet. Rectitude urges Christine to choose the women who will people the new city, and, on Christine's query, names the great ladies of France who deserve to be honoured for all their excellent qualities. Not only great and noble ladies shall live there but excellent women from all estates. Justice's first choice of someone to govern the city is the Blessed Virgin, and Mary accepts the invitation. Finally, Christine addresses the assembly of women, telling them the city is theirs as a protection and a defence against their enemies. She warns them also to be sure to continue in virtue, and not to let their new position make them proud.

In *Le Livre des Trois Vertus* Christine treats of the Female Members of the Body Politic, according to their positions in society – first, princesses and great ladies, second, other women and girls who live at the court, and third, all other ranks of women. She dedicated it to the Dauphinée Margaret. Her interest in women's role and women's affairs lasted till her death, and though the exact date of her death is not known, her last poem is a tribute to Joan of Arc, dated 31 July 1429, written in great joy at the brave actions of this sixteen-year-old girl who earlier that year had ensured the coronation of the dauphin Charles at Rheims. Much of Christine's writing remains as yet largely unjudged by literary criticism. It is certain, though, that she was a remarkable and a prolific writer most highly regarded in her own day, and dedicated to championing women's interests in her society.

I I

Women as Patrons
of Literature

———◆———

Though women's individual contribution to literature and
scholarship may not have been large in volume in the Middle
Ages, they did contribute in another way which was significant
and important. They exercized their powers of patronage. In
the pre-Conquest period in England, lay-women rather than
men featured as owners of books (Wormald, p. 98). Women in
general, freed by virtue of their sex from the necessity of making
war and thus from spending their youth in acquiring martial
arts, had more time to devote to educated and literary pursuits.
Hild, abbess of Whitby, and Radegund, foundress of Poitiers,
are both remembered for their interest in poetic endeavour.

Hild is famous for having encouraged the poetic powers of
Cædmon. Cædmon was a worker on the monastic estate who
was unable to sing when the harp was passed around the table
at a feast. He was given the gift of song in a dream, and urged to
'sing about the creation of all things' (Bede, IV, 24). The
abbess was consulted and, to test him, a passage of scripture
was explained to him, and he was asked to make it into verse.
He had done this by the following morning, and so Hild
persuaded him to abandon secular life and join the monastic
community. She contrived to have him instructed in sacred
history; he was able to meditate on it and turn it into 'such
melodious verse that his delightful renderings turned his in-
structors into his audience'. He made poetry from the Old
Testament and the New, all the more remarkable because it
was 'in his own English tongue' (Bede, IV, 24). He did this by
thinking over the sacred scriptures, 'as though a clean animal,

by ruminating'. This rumination on the word of God, so much advocated by the Rule of St Benedict, is probably the foundation on which surviving Old English biblical poetry was written, for it indicates a deep knowledge not only of the Bible, but sometimes of biblical commentary also. Apart from a brief hymn none of Cædmon's verse has survived.

Radegund, foundress of the nunnery of the Holy Cross at Poitiers, was also enlightened enough to encourage a poet. Venantius Fortunatus was an Italian who had fled from the attacks of the Langobards in 568. After travelling widely he settled at Poitiers and became very friendly with Radegund. His poetry combined cultured Latinity with theology. The presence of the relic of the Holy Cross at Poitiers probably inspired his two most famous hymns – *Pange Lingua* (Sing, my tongue, the Glorious Battle) and *Vexilla Regis* (The Royal Banners forward go). He wrote poetry to Radegund and for Radegund, often in terms which suggest a secular lover, certainly expressive of great friendship and strong affection. He may have taught her to write verse also, for one or two poems formerly attributed to him could well be by Radegund herself. He became bishop of Poitiers towards the end of the sixth century, and drafted the story of her life. Radegund also influenced Gregory of Tours to write about her and her foundation. His *Historia Francorum* contains a lot of information about the nunnery. His *De Gloria Confessorum* tells how he officiated at her death. His *De Gloria Martyrum* mentions the fragment of the Holy Cross which Radegund received from Constantinople, from which the foundation took its name.

In some cases, as in that of Hild and Cædmon, tutelage as much as patronage was involved. Such must also have been the case with Abbess Gerberga and Hrotswitha. Hrotswitha's interest and ability sprang from good teaching, and the teacher in turn encouraged the work of the mature pupil and brought it to the attention of others.

On the whole, however, it is to the later Middle Ages that we must look for evidence of this further branch of literacy amongst women: their patronage consisted in the ability to read or be read to with the eye or ear of a connoisseur, and in the perception of what was worthwhile amongst literary works, backed by the capacity to pay for such luxury items. From the twelfth century onwards a great deal of literature was commissioned by the women of the more cultured aristocracy. There is a sense in which they may be said to have invented literary patronage. The two wives of Henry I (1070–1135) are an example of the phenomenon. For the first, Maud or Matilda (1080–1118), Benedeit wrote the AN *Voyage of Saint Brendan*. For the second, Adela of Louvain (d.1151), Phillippe de Thaon wrote his *Bestiaire*. Adela also patronized Geoffroi Gaimar and David the Trouvère. Maud's is the first known name of a patron of French literature. Her generosity to poets and musicians was well known. She was herself an educated and literate lady, whose surviving letters to Anselm betoken both her own scholarship and her friendship for the man. She also wrote a letter to Pope Pascal (Anselm, V, pp. 253–4).

Maud lived at the beginning of a period when it was possible for an increasing, though still relatively small, number of people outside the Church's officers to be literate, either for pleasure, or for scholarship, or for business purposes. Another early woman patron of letters was Berenguella, Castilian wife of Alfonso IX of Leon. She commissioned the *Chronicon Mundi* of Bishop Lucas of Tuy (el Tudense) in the early thirteenth century. That cultivated reading was within the grasp of noblewomen is evidenced by such wills as that of Eleanor de Bohun, wife of Thomas duke of Gloucester (dated 1399). She left several books to her children, all in French except for Latin psalters. Elizabeth, countess of Salisbury, possessed the French *Historia Scholastica* taken from King John at Poitiers in 1356. In 1377 the Earl of Devon left a French book to one of his daughters (Deanesly, p. 351).

Educated women probably set the whole tone of literature in the courts of southern France in the late eleventh and twelfth centuries; they are patrons in that they called forth a whole genre of love poems, the lyrics of the troubadours. The name of Eleanor of Aquitaine, herself a direct descendant of Guilhem the Ninth, duke of Aquitaine and earliest recorded troubadour, is associated with literary patronage in her native south, and also in the north, whither she went on her marriage to Louis VII of France, and later still in England after she married Henry II. Thomas of Britain's *Tristan and Iseult* may have been written for her, and she is possibly the noble lady to whom Benoît de Sainte-More dedicated his romance of Troy. Wace dedicated his *Brut* to her. For a time she held court at Poitiers, when her husband, Henry II of England, made their eleven-year-old son Richard duke of Aquitaine. Eleanor was duchess of Aquitaine in her own right, and she was the real ruler during a period from 1167 to 1174, presiding over a circle of literary enthusiasts, especially where love poetry was concerned. It is possible that her two daughters had still more influential careers as patrons. Alix married Count Thibaut of Blois in 1164, the same year in which her sister Marie married his brother Count Henry the Liberal of Champagne.

The court of Champagne resided at Troyes, and it was one of the most prolific literary centres in twelfth-century France. Henry the Liberal was himself a great patron of letters, and one of the most famous poets of medieval French literature, Chrétien de Troyes, wrote for this court at this period. In 1181 Count Henry died, leaving Marie to act as regent for their sons, and there certainly followed a period of great literary activity. Conan de Béthune sang there, the poet Gace Brulé was one of her vassals, Auboin de Sézanne wrote for her. Though Chrétien de Troyes is a shadowy figure from the historical point of view (Benton, p. 561), two passages in his works link him with the court of Champagne. He uses the cognomen 'de Troies' in *Erec* 1.9, and in *Lancelot* he states:

> Puis que ma dame de Chanpaigne
> vialt que romans a feire anpraigne,
> je l'anprendrai molt volentiers
> come cil qui est suens antiers

de quan qu'il puet el monde feire. . . .
Mes tant dirai ge que mialz oevre
ses comandemanz an ceste oevre
que sans ne painne que g'i mete.
Del Chevalier de la charrete
comance Crestiens son livre;
matiere et san li done et livre
la contesse, et il s'antremet
de panser, que geures n'i met
fors sa painne et s'antancion. (1–29)

(Since my lady the countess of Champagne wishes me to undertake a romance, I will undertake it willingly, as one who is entirely hers in all that he is capable of on this earth. . . . But for my own part I will only say this much, that her command does more for this work of mine, than any intelligence or effort that I might put into it. Chrétien commences his book of the Knight of the Cart. The countess supplies him with his narrative material and [moral] significance, and he on his part has it clear in his mind that he hardly contributes more than his effort and his attention.)

It is widely believed that Chrétien was less than enamoured with his *Lancelot*, and that in these lines he is excusing himself from complete responsibility for the subject matter (*matière*) and controlling purpose (*san*). It has even been suggested that the adulterous affair between Lancelot and Guinivere was invented by Chrétien to satisfy some notion of love held by Marie (Loomis, p. 178).

During Marie's regency the long poetical paraphrase of the psalm *Eructavit* was written, its author unknown to us. It gives an extended moral and allegorical gloss to a biblical text, quoting a Latin verse and then supplying paraphrase and commentary in French (see Benton, p. 566). *Eructavit cor meum* is Psalm 44 of the Vulgate text, a poem of joy and part of the liturgy of Christmas morning. This psalm symbolized the marriage of Christ and the Church, and the French poem emphasizes divine love and joy, and comments on human marriage. As such it is possible to place it within a general upsurge of love poetry, which flourished in northern France at this period, nowhere more strongly than in Champagne. That poetry celebrated both divine and human love, and Leclerq indicates how closely the two were allied when he links Chrétien de Troyes with St Bernard of Clairvaux, calling them 'the two greatest poets of the garden of love, Champagne' (Leclerq, 1979, p. 121). To express the love of God which takes up within itself all other manifestations of love on earth, St Bernard often drew on the vocabulary of human love, and that of chivalry and warfare, for he was addressing an audience of young men from a milieu which would have understood such concepts. In turn both religious and courtly literature in twelfth-century France received inspiration from him (Leclerq, 1979, p. 107). It is possible to fit *Eructavit* into this background. Religious in content and spiritually instructive in purpose, it expresses the joys of divine love, and was presented to a powerful lay-woman, Marie of Champagne, who is addressed directly in the dedication and conclusion. In the closing decade of the twelfth century a verse translation of Genesis was written by another poet, probably a cleric, called Evrat, at the request of Marie. He was clearly well read in biblical exegesis, and provides an allegorical and moral gloss to his verse translation. Since his text is Genesis, he takes the opportunity to interpret the Fall (he is unfavourable towards Eve's role) and to speak of the sanctity of human marriage. He makes it clear that the work was destined for Marie's court, and also states that she herself would be able to read and understand it, and read it in her library (Benton, p. 564).

The once widely held view that Andreas Capellanus, author of the famous treatise *De Arte Honeste Amandi* or *De Amore*, usually translated as 'The Art of Courtly Love' was Marie's chaplain (*capellanus*) is no longer a matter of certainty. The most important manuscript evidence from the work itself suggests that he was at the royal court (Benton, p. 578). No external evidence supports these suggestions. However, there is evidence in Countess Marie's charters between 1182 and 1186 that an 'Andreas Capellanus' was an important member of her court. His title of *Dominus* shows that this Andreas or Andrew was a priest. Nothing else is known of him (Rajna, pp. 193ff.).

The Andreas of the *De Amore* claims personal knowledge about Marie and cites a letter from her dated 1174, giving a 'judgement' in a love problem. Much weight has been given to this as evidence of communication between Andreas and Countess Marie. Yet the possibility that Andreas was in Marie's employ and wrote for her is not the only problem. It has not yet been resolved and probably never will be finally settled whether *De Amore* is a serious account of love practices in courtly society in the late twelfth century, or an imaginative work, humorous and ironic, taking to the ultimate degree ideas about love already to be found in twelfth-century secular literature. However, its procedure of question and answer, its legal casebook presentation, and its threefold structure, the last section completely rebutting all the special pleadings of the first two sections, suggest a conscious literary creation rather than an historical document. Marie's 'judgements' in love problems are cited more than once, but in what appears to be the quotation of the full text of a letter, she judges that:

> love cannot exert its powers between two people who are married to each other. For lovers give each other everything freely, under no compulsion or necessity, but married people are in duty bound to give in to each other's desires and deny themselves to each other in nothing. (Andreas Capellanus, pp. 106–7)

Benton shrewdly points out (p. 590) that if Marie's convictions and those of her circle had in reality been so subversive of the right relationship between husband and wife some criticism (or even praise) of this waywardness would have found its place in the large body of literature which can be associated without doubt with her court. Not even the sermon preached by the Cistercian, Adam de Perseigne, on her deathbed can lay anything other than conventional human vanity and worldly pride to her account (Benton, pp. 582 and 588). To see Andreas or indeed Chrétien as satirists and moralists is rather to enhance the sophistication of the intellectual milieu for which they wrote. By comparison latter-day believers in Andreas' literalness appear excessively credulous. There are no real reasons for supposing that Andreas, any more than Chrétien, was a social historian. The manuscript evidence would indicate that Andreas' work was not widely known in the twelfth century (by comparison with, for example, St Bernard's commentary on the Song of Songs which was the twelfth-century equivalent of a best-seller) so the *De Amore* is certainly not a reliable guide to the kind of writing that would have found favour with a twelfth-century audience (Leclerq, 1979, p. 118).

Marie and the literary circle created and fostered by her (and her husband) are an outstanding example of literary patronage in any century, their widely spread tastes embracing romances, lyric poetry, religious treatises and scriptural exegesis. Few, if any, names of queens or noblewomen after the twelfth century in England can be cited to illustrate women's interest in literary patronage. However, the importance of women to writers in court circles is probably indicated in the fourteenth century by such things as Chaucer's concern for the reaction of the women in his audience to the story of Criseyde's unfaithfulness in his *Troilus and Criseyde*:

> Besechyng every lady bright of hewe,
> And every gentil womman, what she be
> That al be that Criseyde was untrewe,
> That for that gilt she be not wroth with me.
> Ye may hire giltes in other bokes se;
> And gladlier I wol write, yif yow leste
> Penelopees trouthe and good Alceste.
>
> N'y sey nat this al oonly for thise men,
> But mooste for wommen that bitraised be
> Thorugh false folk; God yeve hem sorwe, Amen!
> That with hire grete wit and subtilte
> Bytraise yow! And this commeveth me

> To speke, and in effect, yow alle I preye,
> Beth war of men, and herkneth what I seye! (V, 1772–85)

(Begging every lady lovely of complexion and every noblewoman whoever she may be, that, although Criseyde was unfaithful, she is not angry with me, on account of that sin. You may see her sins in other books, and I will write all the more willingly, if it pleases you, of the fidelity of Penelope and of good Alceste. I do not say this only for these men, but mainly for women who are betrayed through false people; God give them sorrow, Amen! who betray you with their great wit and subtlety. And this moves me to speak, and in effect I pray you all to beware of men and listen to what I say!)

In the *Legend of Good Women* the God of Love accuses Chaucer of saying *wikednesse* about women.

> Was there no good matere in thy mynde,
> Ne in alle thy bokes me coudest thow nat fynde
> Som story of wemen that were goode and trewe? (G. 270–2)

Lydgate also apologizes for the harsh treatment of women in his *Troy Book* (R. W. Frank, p. 84).

Late medieval examples of royal or noblewomen patronizing learning in general are found in the involvement of women in certain university colleges. Margaret of Anjou, wife of Henry VI (1421–61, himself the founder of King's College, Cambridge), was allowed by her husband to refound and rename St Bernard's College, Cambridge. After the deposition of Henry VI, Elizabeth, the wife of his successor, Edward IV (1443–83), continued Margaret's work. The apostrophe after *s* in the name of Queens' College indicates that it regards itself as having been founded by both queens. Lady Margaret Beaufort, mother of Henry VII, founded both Christ's College and St John's College in Cambridge. Lady Margaret actually died before the foundation of St John's in 1511, but she was responsible for the taking over of a small college called God's House (founded 1439) and renaming it Christ's College in 1505. She took great interest in the development of the College and its statutes, and frequently stayed there. This late reflex of women's interest in foundations of learning presents a marked difference from that displayed in earlier centuries. Earlier, women had founded or endowed monasteries as havens of learning for their own sex, or at least for both sexes. In the fifteenth and early sixteenth centuries they are found to be patronizing learning establishments exclusively for men. With this proviso, learning as a whole was being patronized more than single authors and individual works. The activity of these royal women is a relief after a couple of centuries in which queens of England were either totally unremarkable in any respect, or threw themselves wholeheartedly into political intrigue, on behalf of, or sometimes against, their royal husbands. However, it was the noble women of the eleventh and twelfth centuries who had given literary patronage a status which set a standard and a pattern for all patrons of the arts for many centuries to come.

Conclusion

———◆———

It is relatively straightforward to survey some of the information to be found about women in the Middle Ages as it appears in contemporary sources, but not so easy to come to conclusions, much less generalizations about the realities of woman's lot during that long period. There is no denying the theoretically well-developed limitations of the female, running from the moral condemnation of Eve's transgression to the scientific beliefs in the inferiority of woman's biological functions. The idea that the female was physically, intellectually and morally weaker than the male is as old as Aristotle (*Historia Animalium*, 608 B). Even in the business of reproducing the species, woman's contribution was small. Woman did not contribute semen to the process of generation, but, according to Aristotle, she provided the menstrual blood, out of which the embryo was made:

> Thus, if the male is the active partner, the one who originates the movement, and the female *qua* female is the passive one, surely what the female contributes to the semen of the male will be not semen but material. And this is in fact what we find happening; for the natural substance of the menstrual fluid is to be classed as 'prime matter'. (Aristotle, *Generation of Animals*, 129a, 25–34)

That the female provided exactly half of the foetus' genetic message was not known. It seemed more plausible to consider woman merely as a 'host', nursing the child in her womb until the time of birth. To this extent she was not fully a parent; the parent was the male.

Those living in the medieval world were a little kinder than the Ancients. Albertus Magnus (1206–80) spoke of the woman's seed, though he believed it suffered coagulation – like cheese – by the male seed, and also believed that the menstrual blood played a part (Needham, p. 87, quoting Albertus Magnus' *De Generatione Animalium*). Thomas Aquinas' statements are perhaps the most clear. He believed that the generative power of the female was imperfect compared to that of the male. 'Corporeal matter . . . is supplied by the mother', while the 'active seminal power' is from the father (Thomas Aquinas, *Summa*, pt.I, q.cxix, art.2). He also writes:

> Now in generation there are two distinct operations – that of the agent and that of the patient. Wherefore it follows that the entire active operation is on the part of the male, and the passive on the part of the female. (Thomas Aquinas, *Summa*, pt.III, q.xxxii, art.4)

However, a female child was not the result of defective procreation, as Aristotle would have argued (Aristotle, *Generation of Animals*, 766a, 20–30; see also Bullough, 1973, p. 487). Woman was part of God's plan. But she had to submit to her superior, man, for the sake of good order, 'because in man the discretion of reason predominates' (Thomas Aquinas, *Summa*, pt.I, q.xcii, art.1). It is not without significance that such women as are known to have involved themselves with this area of study either concerned themselves with the mystical problem of the ensoulment of the foetus as did Hildegard of Bingen in her *Scivias* (see Needham, p. 84) or with the more practical considerations of gynaecology and obstetrics, like Trotula, a matron of Salerno. To Trotula is usually ascribed *De Passionibus Mulierum*. Needham mentions the tradition that Salernitan women taught obstetrics at the School of Salerno and that the name of one woman professor has come down to us, that of Costanza Calenda of Salerno, who lectured at Naples sometime in the fourteenth century (p. 86).

Thus there were widely held views both theological and scientific which could be used to explain the reasons for the inferior position of women in medieval society. Such attitudes did not prevent women from fulfilling a useful and worthwhile role in society, but to find out what that role was it is necessary to turn from the theorists to the poets and historians and to the personal letters, where they survive. It would appear that providing she lived within the rules and ideas which society believed to be appropriate to her station – maiden, wife or consecrated virgin – a woman had a fair degree of freedom of action. Even amongst the upper classes, she was not a harem-style recluse, and amongst the labouring classes she was always expected to do her share of the work on the land and in the town (Power, 1975, pp. 53ff.). In Anglo-Saxon times a woman could wield power even beneath a nun's veil. In political life there are examples like that of Seaxburh, widow of Coenwalh of Wessex, who ruled for a year after her husband's death. Æthelflæd, King Alfred's daughter, ruled West Mercia jointly with her husband till he died in 911, and after that ruled alone, acquiring the title 'Lady of the Mercians', the exact equivalent of her late husband's name of 'Lord of the Mercians'. Ælfgifu, first wife of Canute, ruled Norway on behalf of her son Swein and was so unpopular that they were both forced to leave the country. She later persuaded England to accept her son Harold as king after the death of Canute. Anglo-Saxon women owned land, as is evidenced by place-names bearing a woman's name, such as Babraham and Wilbraham (Cambs.), which contain the names Beaduburg and Wilburg (see F. Stenton, pp. 5ff.). Women could also bequeath land as well as other possessions as they pleased.

The Norman Conquest introduced restrictions on woman's independence which had not been evident in Anglo-Saxon times, both in relation to marriage and in regard to her power in the cloister. The women of England may have settled down to experiencing Norman ways more quickly than their menfolk, for it is no more than logical to assume that the earliest inter-marriages taking place were those between Anglo-Saxon women and Norman males who had come alone to England. Name-evidence seems to suggest that this is so, in that it quickly became fashionable to give sons continental names, such as Robert, William and Gilbert, presumably after their fathers' families'. names, whereas women's names retained an Anglo-Saxon bias for quite some time, even in 'normanized' forms such as Ailiva and Brichtiva (Æthelgifu and Beorhtgifu, see Clark, pp. 223ff.). Anglo-Saxon men's names fell quite rapidly in popularity in the post-Conquest period even amongst the peasant and middle classes, and not just amongst the nobility (Clark, p. 234). It is probably fair to say that it was in large measure through these insular wives and mothers of Anglo-Norman children that the English language was preserved and soon became familiar to a large number of the French-speaking ruling class. In this regard, not only noble matrons must take credit, but also a host of nameless nurses, nannies, waiting-women and servants, whose presence would have been essential to the running of a noble household (see Clark, p. 231).

Feudal tenancies were only exceptionally held by women, and so women's names appear less frequently in post-Conquest records. This change was not immediate. The Domesday Book shows women holding lands, not just as widows, but holding separate estates during the life of their husbands, estates which the husband had no power to give or sell. But under William Rufus (1087–1100) change became more general (Buckstaff, p. 55). Then, the feudal system of holding all land in return for service really took root and the king became the guardian of women and children. Anglo-Norman women were rarely called upon to witness charters or to grant lands to nunneries, as they had reduced rights to hold land and make wills. A woman was entitled to one-third of what her husband possessed when she married him, no matter how much he acquired later on. During her marriage she had no rights over her dower, which her husband managed and could alienate without her consent. Indeed, if it could be proved against her that she had opposed her husband in the sale of her dower, she could have no claim on the buyer of 'her' property after her husband's death (Pollock and Maitland, II, 423).

Even if she did not object at the time, she would have to go through a legal process to get her dower if it was not vacant. A writ specially designed to enable the widow to recover land alienated by her husband is, in both England and Normandy, one of the oldest writs (Pollock and Maitland, II, 410). The heir could dispute her claim to her dower, and so cause her further complications (Buckstaff, p. 52, citing Glanvill, Henry II's Justiciar). Some of these harsh measures were softened in the course of time. Magna Carta ensured that a widow would be provided with one third of all the land her husband possessed in his life (Pollock and Maitland, II, 421). By the reign of Edward IV (1461–83), a husband could bequeath more than one third or even the whole of his land to his wife (Buckstaff, p. 60).

Of course the most powerful in the land were free of even the worst of these strictures. William the Conqueror's queen, Matilda, and Henry I's queens, Maud and Adela, held and administered great estates, they had their own officers and chancellors, and occasionally acted as regent in the King's absence. Matilda, wife of Stephen (1135–54), likewise conducted her own affairs. Eleanor of Aquitaine was able to move her great inheritance from spouse to spouse and back to her own keeping with as much ease as if she had lived a century or two earlier. Her duchy added immensely to the kingdom of France, well nigh doubling that realm, when she married Louis VII. When she divorced him and married Henry II of England, her land went with her. After she quarrelled with Henry, she retired to Aquitaine and set up her second son as her heir (the eldest being destined for the English throne).

Such examples would have kept alive, even in the darkest Norman days, the possibility that a capable woman would always be able to manage her own – and sometimes her husband's – affairs when the opportunity presented itself. By the time that Bracton was writing his *Notebook* in the mid-thirteenth century, a woman could hold land, own chattels and make a will, make a contract, sue and be sued. She could plead in her own person, without intermediary, even appear as her husband's attorney (Pollock and Maitland, I, 482). A widow could be the guardian of her own children, a lady could be guardian of her tenants' children. However, women were excluded from all public functions. 'In the camp, at the Council board, on the bench, in the jury box there is no place for them' (Pollock and Maitland, I, 485).

The rising middle classes produced women who did not fit into any of the moulds cast by early Anglo-Norman society. Working women became more numerous, especially in the towns, carrying on trade on their own, or working as the assistants of their craftsmen husbands (Power, 1975, p. 53). At the end of the fourteenth century, Chaucer, himself not of the aristocratic milieu for which he wrote, presented us with that strong and independent weaver, the Wife of Bath, and the well-off, showy, self-important wives of the five guildsmen. Even the Prioress has a wilful independent streak, despite her gracious manners, or she would not be on pilgrimage. That women were still to be viewed as objects of exploitation or creatures to be mistrusted is shown in Chaucer's presentation within the *Canterbury Tales* of the treacherous yet ill-used May, the bland undelineated Emelye and the foolish Dorigen, yet strength and heroism are shown in the stories of Griselda and Constance and in the saintly Cecilia. In the fifteenth century, Lydgate was able to feel compassion for women as sentient beings in his *Temple of Glas* where he shows the plight of one whose passions have to be suppressed because convention demands it. Yet Lydgate's clerical calling can permit him in other works to take a more clerkly anti-feminist approach to womankind, marvelling at the stupidity of foolish men who give faith or credence to any woman (Lydgate, *Troy Book*, I, 1847–8; see Renoir, pp. 9–13). It is thus difficult to paint an overall picture which shows lack of sympathy for women, much less grossly inferior treatment of the sex. In general, a woman remained free within her given domains. The wife's powers in her own province had been indicated in Anglo-Saxon times by the law of Canute which stated her power and duty to guard the keys of her storeroom, chest and cupboard (Robertson, pp. 212–13). Throughout the Middle Ages a woman ran her household or business, often singlehanded, with her menfolk away at war or on crusade. Later centuries give examples of women of the gentry like the Pastons, who continued over many generations to manage household, estate and family business in their husbands' prolonged absences. Such instances must stand as convincing evidence that, in spite of legal restrictions, in the detailed concerns of everyday life, many women were neither regarded as useless nor were they oppressed, and that they were often accorded considerable responsibility.

Select Bibliography

◆

The Select Bibliography, intended as a reference guide to the texts and studies referred to by author and/or title in the course of the book, including translations, is divided into six parts, A–F. Section A deals with works cited throughout the text, and is followed by separate sections for references from each section of the book, including the Conclusion (B–E). Section F lists some works which may be of interest for further reading. Authors are listed in alphabetical order in each section. Abbreviated titles are given in brackets after entries where necessary.

A *Works Cited Throughout*

Abelard, *Epistles*, ed. J. T. Muckle and T. P. McLaughlin, *MS*, 12 (1950), 163–213, 15 (1953), 47–94, 17 (1955), 240–281, 18 (1956), 241–292; also PL CLXXVIII, 113–380.

The Apocrypha of the Old Testament, cited from the Revised Standard Version (Oxford, 1957 edn), *Third and Fourth Books of the Maccabees and Psalm 151* (Oxford, 1977 edn).

Augustine of Hippo, *De Bono Coniugali* 'The good of Marriage', ed. P. Schaff in NPNF III, 397–413. *(De Bono Con.)*

Bede, *A History of the English Church and People*, trans. L. Sherley-Price (Harmondsworth, 1955).

Chaucer, Geoffrey, *The Complete Works of Geoffrey Chaucer*, ed. F. N. Robinson, 2nd edn (Oxford, 1957).

Chaucer, Geoffrey, *The General Prologue to The Canterbury Tales*, ed. P. Hodgson (London, 1969).

Chaucer, Geoffrey, *The Merchant's Prologue and Tale*, ed. M. Hussey (Cambridge, 1965).

Chaucer, Geoffrey, *The Wife of Bath's Prologue and Tale*, ed. J. Winny (Cambridge, 1965).

Eckenstein, L., *Woman under Monasticism* (Cambridge, 1896).
Gratian, *Corpus Juris Canonici*, ed. E. Friedberg, I, *Decretum* (Leipzig, 1879).
Gregory of Tours, *The History of the Franks*, trans. L. Thorpe (Harmondsworth, 1974).
Hali Meidenhad, ed. F. J. Furnivall, EETS, o.s. 18 (1922, Repr. 1969).
The Holy Bible, cited from the Revised Standard Version (Oxford, 1952–71).
Jerome, *Epistola adversus Jovinianum*, Libri III, PL XXIII, 211–338. *(Ad. Jov.)*
Langland, William, *Piers Plowman: the B Version*, ed. G. Kane and E. T. Donaldson (London, 1975).
Langland, William, *Piers Plowman, An Edition of the C-text*, ed. D. Pearsall (London, 1978).
Leclerq, J., *Monks and Love in Twelfth Century France* (Oxford, 1979).
Lorris, Guillaume de, see *Roman de la Rose*.
Meun, Jean de, see *Roman de la Rose*.
Ovid, *Ars Amatoria*, 'The Art of Love', trans. J. H. Mozley, in *Works* 2nd edn (London, 1979).
The Paston Letters and Papers of the Fifteenth Century, ed. N. Davis, I–II (Oxford, 1971 and 1976).
Power, E., *Medieval English Nunneries* (Cambridge, 1922).
Le Roman de La Rose 'The Romance of the Rose' by Guillaume de Lorris and Jean de Meun, ed. C. W. Dunn, trans. H. W. Robbins (New York, 1962).
Utley, F. L., *The Crooked Rib* (New York, 1970).
Whitelock, D., ed. and trans., *Anglo-Saxon Wills* (Cambridge, 1930).

B *Women and Religion*

Abelard, *Expositio in Hexameron*, PL CLXXVIII, 729–84. *(Hex.)*
Abelard, *Sermo in Assumptione B. Mariae*, Sermo XXVI in PL CLXXVIII, 539–47.
Adam of Courlandon, *Allegoriae Morales*, quoted from manuscript by d'Alverny, 1977.
Alan of Lille, *Liber in Distinctionibus – dictionum theologicalium*, PL CCX, 687–1012. *(Distinct.)*
Aldhelm, *De Laudibus Virginitatis*, ed. J. A. Giles in *Aldhelm, Opera Omnia* (Oxford, 1884), pp. 1–82. *(De Laud. Virg.)*

Aldhelm, *De Octo Principalibus Vitiis*, ed. J. A. Giles in *Aldhelm, Opera Omnia* (Oxford, 1884), pp. 203–15.

d'Alverny, M.-T., *Alain de Lille, Textes Inédites* (Paris, 1965).

d'Alverny, M.-T., 'Comment les Theologiens et les Philosophes voient la femme', *Cahiers de Civilisation Mediévales*, 20 (1977), 105–29.

Ambrose, *De Paradiso* 'Paradise', trans. J. J. Savage in FC XLII, 287–356. *(De Par.)*

Ambrose, *De Virginibus* 'Virgins', ed. P. Schaff and H. Wace in NPNF, 2nd Series X, pp. 361–87. *(De Virg.)*

Ambrose, *Hexameron* 'The Creation', trans. J. J. Savage in FC XLII, 3–283.

Ancrene Riwle, 'The Nun's Rule', trans. J. Morton (London, 1905).

Andrew of St Victor, *Commentarium in Genesim*, quoted from manuscript by d'Alverny, 1977.

The Anglo-Saxon Chronicle, trans. D. Whitelock, D. C. Douglas, and S. I. Tucker (London, 1961).

Anselm, *Cur Deus Homo*, ed. F. S. Schmitt in *Anselmi Opera* (Edinburgh, 1946–61), II, 37–133.

Anselm, *De Conceptu Virginali*, ed. F. S. Schmitt in *Anselmi Opera* (Edinburgh, 1946–61), II, 135–73. *(De Con. Virg.)*

Augustine of Hippo, *De Genesi ad Litteram*, Libri XII, PL XXXIV, 245–486. *(De Gen. ad Litt.)*

Augustine of Hippo, *De Genesi contra Manichaeos*, Libri II, PL XXXIV, 173–220. *(De Gen. Contra Man.)*

Augustine of Hippo, *De Sancta Virginitate* 'Holy Virginity', ed. P. Schaff in NPNF III, 418–438. *(De Sancta Virg.)*

Augustine of Hippo, *De Trinitate* 'The Trinity', ed. P. Schaff in NPNF III, 17–228.

Augustine of Hippo, *In Joannis Evangelium* 'On the Gospel of St John', ed. P. Schaff in NPNF VII, 7–452.

The Battle of Maldon, ed. E. v K. Dobbie in ASPR VI, trans. in D. Whitelock, EHD I, pp. 319–24.

Bernard of Clairvaux, *Sermo Dominica infra Octavam Assumptionis*, ed. J. Leclerq o.s.b., C. H. Talbot, and H. M. Rochais o.s.b. in *Works* (Rome, 1957–), V, 262–274.

Bernard of Clairvaux, *Sermo in Nativitate B. Mariae*, ed. Leclerq o.s.b. et al. in *Works* V, 275–288.

Bernard of Clairvaux, *(Sermons) On the Song of Songs*, trans. and ed. by a religious of C.S.M.V. (London, 1952).

Bullough, V. L., 'The Prostitute in the Middle Ages', *Studies in Medieval Culture*, 10 (1977), 9–17.

Chodorow, S., *Christian Political Theory and Church Politics in the Mid-Twelfth Century. The Ecclesiology of Gratian's Decretum* (Berkeley, 1972).

Cyprian, *De Habitu Virginum* 'The Dress of Virgins', trans. R. J. Deferrari in FC XXXVI, 31–52. *(De Hab. Virg.)*

Eriugena, John Scotus, *Periphiseon (De Divisione Naturae)*, Libri V, PL CXXII, 441–1022.

Ernaud of Bonneval, *Hexaemeron (De Operibus Sex Dierum)*, PL CLXXXIX, 1513–1570. *(Hex.)*

Ferrante, J. M., *Woman as Image in Medieval Literature from the Twelfth Century to Dante* (New York, 1975).

Genesis B, ed. G. P. Krapp in ASPR I.

Geoffrey of Vendôme, *Epistolae*, Libri V, PL CLVII, 34–212.

Godstow Nunnery, The English Register of, ed. A. Clark, EETS o.s. 129, 130, 142 (1905–11, Repr. 1971).

Gray, D., *A Selection of Religious Lyrics* (Oxford, 1975).

Gregory of Nyssa, *De Hominis Opificio 'La Création de l'Homme'*, trans. J. Laplace, notes by J. Daniélou, SC VI (1944). *(De Hom. Op.)*

Hirn, Y., *The Sacred Shrine, A Study of the Poetry and Art of the Catholic Church* (London, 1958).

Hugh of St Victor, *De Sacramentis Christianae Fidei*, Prologus and Libri II, PL CLXXVI, 173–618. *(De Sac. Ch. Fid.)*

Isidore of Seville, *De Ecclesiasticis Officiis*, Libri II, PL LXXXIII, 737–826. *(De Eccles. Officiis)*

Isidore of Seville, *Sententiae*, Libri III, PL LXXXIII, 537–738. *(Sent.)*

Isidore of Seville, *Etymologiae*, Libri XX, PL LXXXII, 73–728. *(Etym.)*

Jerome, *Commentarius in Ecclesiasten*, PL XXIII, 1009–1116. *(In Eccles.)*

Jerome, *Letter to Eustochium*, Letter XXII in *Letters of St Jerome*, trans. C. C. Mierow in ACW XXXIII, 134–179.

Le Jeu d'Adam, ed. W. Noomen (Paris, 1971), esp. pp. 43–53.

Labrolle, P. de., *History and Literature of Christianity from Tertullian to Boethius* (London and New York, 1924).

Lyndwood, W., *Provinciale (Seu Constitutiones Angliae)*, with commentary by John of Ayton (Oxford, 1679).

Marbod of Rennes, *Epistolae*, PL CLXXI, 1465–92.

Meyer, M. A., 'Women and the Tenth Century English Monastic Reform', *RB*, 87 (1977), 34–61.

Muckle, see Abelard.

Le Mystère d'Adam, see *Le Jeu d'Adam*.

Peter Comestor, *Distinctiones*, quoted from manuscript by d'Alverny, 1977.

Philo of Alexandria, *De Opificio Mundi* 'On the Account of the World's Creation given by Moses', trans. F. H. Colson and G. H. Whitaker, in *Works* (London, 1929, Repr. 1962), I, 6–137. *(De Op. Mundi)*

Philo of Alexandria, *Legum Allegoria* 'Allegorical Interpretation of Genesis II, III,' trans. F. H. Colson and G. H. Whitaker, in *Works* (London, 1929, Repr. 1962), I, 146–473. *(Legum)*

The Regularis Concordia, ed. T. Symons (London, 1953).

Rupert of Deutz, *Commentarium in Genesim*, ed. H. Haacke o.s.b. in *De Sancta Trinitate et operibus eius*, CCCM XXI, 129–578. *(In Genesim)*

Smith, J., 'Robert of Arbrissel's Relations with Women', in *Medieval Women*, ed. D. Baker, SCH, Subsidia I (Oxford, 1978), pp. 175–84.

Tertullian, *De Exhortatione Castitatis* 'An Exhortation to Chastity', trans. W. P. Le Saint s.j. in ACW XIII, 42–64. *(De Exhort. Cast.)*

Tertullian, *De Cultu Feminarum* 'The Apparel of Women', trans. E. A. Quain s.j., in FC XL, 111–49. *(De Cult. Fem.)*

Tertullian, *De Virginibus Velandis*, ed. E. Dekkers in CCSL II, 1209–1226. *(De Virg. Vel.)*

Thomas Aquinas, *Summa Theologiae*, trans. Fathers of the English Dominican Province (London, 1911–).

Thompson, S., 'The Problem of the Cistercian Nuns in the Twelfth and Early Thirteenth Centuries', in *Medieval Women*, ed. D. Baker, SCH, Subsidia I (Oxford, 1978), pp. 227–52.

Tynemouth, John of, *Nova Legenda Anglie*, ed. C. Horstman (Oxford, 1901).

Unrue, J. C., *Hali Meidenhad and other Virginity Treatises* (unpubl. Ph.D. dissertation, Ohio State University, 1970).

Vitry, Jacques de, *Historia Occidentalis* (Bk. II of his *Historia Hierosolimitana Abbreviata*), ed. J. F. Hinnebusch (Fribourg, 1972).

Walter, J. von, 'Die Ersten Wanderprediger Frankreichs', *Studien zur Geschichte der Theologie und der Kirche* IX, 3 (1903), 1–180.

Warner, M., *Alone of All Her Sex: The Myth and Cult of the Virgin Mary* (London, 1976).

Whitelock, D., ed., *English Historical Documents* I, 2nd edn (London, 1979).

William of Malmesbury, *Gesta Pontificum*, ed. N.E.S.A. Hamilton, RS 52 (London, 1870). *(Gesta Pont.)*

Woolf, R., 'The Fall of Man in *Genesis B* and the *Mystère d'Adam*', in *Studies in Old English Literature in Honor of A. G. Brodeur*, ed. S. B. Greenfield (Eugene, 1963), pp. 187–99.

C *Women and Marriage*

Ælfric, *Life of St. Edmund, King and Martyr*, ed. G. I. Needham (London, 1966), pp. 43–59.

Ambrose, *De Abraham*, Libri II, PL XIV, 419–500.

Ambrose, *Expositio Evangelii Secundum Lucam*, PL XV, 1527–1850. *(Luke)*

Amis and Amiloun, ed. MacEdward Leach, EETS, o.s. 203 (1937).

Attenborough, F. L., ed. and trans., *The Laws of the Earliest English Kings* (Cambridge, 1922).

Augustine of Hippo, *De Bono Viduitatis*, 'The Good of Widowhood', ed. P. Schaff in NPNF III, 441–54. *(De Bono Vid.)*

Augustine of Hippo, *De Nuptiis et Concupiscentia*, PL XLIV, 413–474. *(De Nuptiis)*

Beaumanoir, P. de, *Coutumes de Beauvaisis*, ed. A. Salmon (Paris, 1899, Repr. 1970).

Beowulf and The Fight at Finnsburg, ed. F. Klaeber, 3rd edn (Boston, 1950).

The Book of the Knight of the Tower, trans. W. Caxton, ed. M. Y. Offord, EETS, s.s. 2 (1971).

The Book of Vices and Virtues, ed. W. N. Francis, EETS, o.s. 217 (1942).

Bozon, N., *Les Contes Moralisés de Nicole Bozon*, ed. L. Toulmin-Smith and P. Meyer, SATF (1889).

Bozon, N., *Metaphors of Brother Bozon*, trans. by J. R., a Bencher of the Honourable Society of Gray's Inn (London, 1913). *(Metaphs.)*

Bromyard, J., *Summa Praedicantium* (Venice, 1586).

Burrow, J. A., *A Reading of Sir Gawain and the Green Knight* (Oxford, 1965).

Caird, G. B., 'Paul and Women's Liberty', *BJRL*, 54 (1971), 268–81.

Capitularia Regum Francorum, ed. A. Boretius, MGH Leges in Quart II, I (Hannover, 1883). *(Cap. Reg. Franc.)*

Corpus Juris Civilis, III, *Novellae*, ed. R. Schoell and W. Kroll (Berlin, 1954).

Coulton, G. C., *Chaucer and his England*, 8th edn (London, 1950).

Deschamps, E., *Miroir de Mariage*, in G. Raynaud, *Oeuvres Complètes d'Eustache Deschamps*, SATF (1894).

Duby, G., *Medieval Marriage* (Baltimore and London, 1978).

The Durham Ritual, see *Rituale Ecclesiae Dunelmensis*.

Émaré, ed. W. H. French and C. B. Hale, in *Middle English Metrical Romances* (New York, 1930), pp. 423–55.

Frank, R., 'Marriage in Twelfth- and Thirteenth-Century Iceland', *Viator*, 4 (1973), 473–84.

Gautier, L., *La Chevalerie* (Paris, 1884).

The Goodman of Paris, ed. E. E. Power (London, 1928).

Haskell, A. S., 'The Paston Women on Marriage in Fifteenth-Century England', *Viator*, 4 (1973), 459–71.

Helmholtz, R. H., *Marriage Litigation in Medieval England* (London, 1974).

Howard, G. E., *A History of Matrimonial Institutions*, I–III (Chicago and London, 1904).

Hugh of Lincoln, Life of, ed. J. Dimock, RS 37 (1864).

Jerome, *Commentarium in Epistolam B. Pauli ad Ephesios*, PL XXIX, 777–84. *(Ephesians)*

Jerome, *Letter to Amandus*, Epistola IV, in PL XXII, 562–63. *(Amandus)*

Kelly, H. A., 'Clandestine Marriage and Chaucer's *Troilus*', *Viator*, 4 (1973), 435–57.

Kelly, H. A., *Love and Marriage in the Age of Chaucer* (Ithaca and London, 1975).

King Horn, ed. W. H. French and C. B. Hale, in *Middle English Metrical Romances* (New York, 1930), pp. 25–70.

Knight of the Tower, see *Book of*.

Lombard, Peter, *Sententiae*, Libri IIII (Venice, 1578).

McNamara, J. A., and Wemple, S. F., 'Marriage and Divorce in the Frankish Kingdom', in *Women and Medieval Society*, ed. S. M. Stuard (Pennsylvania, 1976), pp. 95–124.

Mannynge, Robert, of Brunne, *Handlyng Synne*, EETS, o.s. 119, 123 (1901–3, Repr. 1973).

Manuale et Processionale ad usum Insignis Eboracensis (York Ritual), SSP LXIII (1874), *Ordo ad faciendum Sponsalia*, pp. 24–40.

Maskell, W., *The Liturgy of the Church of England according to the uses of Sarum, Bangor, York, and Hereford and the Modern Roman Liturgy* arranged in parallel columns (London, 1884, 2nd edn 1846).

Maskell, W., *Monumenta Ritualia Ecclesiae Anglicanae* or Occasional offices of the Church of England according to the ancient use of Salisbury, the Prymer in English and other prayers and forms, I–III (London, 1846–47).

Le Menagier de Paris, see *The Goodman of Paris*, also Section F.

Mirk, John, *Festial*, ed. T. Erbe, EETS, e.s. 96 (1905, Repr. 1973).

Molin, J. B., and Mutembé, P., *Le Rituel Du Marriage en France du XIIe au XVIe Siècle* (Paris, 1974).

Noah, The Play of, see *Processus Noe*.

Noonan, J. T. Jr., 'Marital Affection in the Canonists', *Studia Gratiana: Collectanea Stephan Kuttner*, 12 (1967), 481–509.

Noonan, J. T. Jr., 'Power to Choose', *Viator*, 4 (1973), 419–34.

O'Faolain, J. and Martines, L., *Not in God's Image* (London, 1973).

Oresme, N., *Le Livre de Yconomique d'Aristote*, ed. and trans. A. D. Menut, *TAPS*, n.s. 47, pt. 5 (Philadelphia, 1957).

Owst, G. R., *Literature and Pulpit in Medieval England*, 2nd edn (Oxford, 1961).

Parmisano, F., o.p., 'Love and Marriage in the Middle Ages', *New Blackfriars*, 50 (1969), 599–608 and 649–60.

Peter Lombard, see Lombard.

Pontifical of Egbert in SSP LXIII (1874); Appendix *Ordines ad faciendum Sponsalia* I, p. 157*.

Poole, A. L., *From Domesday Book to Magna Carta 1087–1216*, 2nd edn (Oxford, 1955).

Power, E., *Medieval Women*, ed. M. M. Postan (Cambridge, 1975).

Powicke, F. M., and Cheney, C. R., eds., *Councils and Synods* with other documents relating to the English Church A.D. 1205–1313, II, i, 2 (Oxford, 1964).

Processus Noe cum Filiis, ed. A. C. Cawley in *The Wakefield Pageants in The Towneley Cycle* (Manchester, 1958, Repr. 1963), pp. 14–28.

The Red Boke of Darbye, in SSP LXIII (1874); Appendix, *Ordines ad faciendum Sponsalia* III, p. 159*.

Rituale Ecclesiae Dunelmensis, ed. U. Lindelöf, SSP CXL (1927).

Robertson, A. J., ed. and trans., *The Laws of the Kings of England from Edmund to Henry I* (Cambridge, 1925).

Rolle, Richard, of Hampole, *Incendium Amoris*, ed. M. Deanesly (Manchester, 1915).

Salmon, see Beaumanoir.

Sellar, W. C., and Yeatman, R. J., *1066 And All That* (London, 1930, Repr. 1975).

Sheehan, M. M., c.s.b., 'The Formation and Stability of Marriage in Fourteenth-Century England: Evidence of an Ely Register', *MS*, 33 (1971), 228–63.

Shippey, T. A., *Old English Verse* (London, 1972).

Sir Gawain and The Green Knight, ed. J. R. R. Tolkien and E. V. Gordon, rev. N. Davis (Oxford, 1967).

Smalley, B., *The Study of the Bible in the Middle Ages* (Oxford, 1952).

Smith, C. E., *Papal Enforcement of Some Medieval Marriage Laws* (New York, 1940).

Speculum Laicorum, ed. J. Th. Welter (Paris, 1914).

Spousal Services, see *Manuale*, also *Pontifical of Egbert* and *Red Boke of Darbye*.

Stenton, D. M., *The English Woman in History* (London, 1957).

Tacitus, *De Origine et Situ Germanorum*, ed. J. G. C. Anderson, (Oxford, 1938); also trans. H. Mattingley in *On Britain and Germany* (Harmondsworth, 1948). *(Germania)*

Torquemada, see Turrecremata.

Turrecremata, J. De, *In Gratiani Decretorum Primam (– Tertiam Partem) Commentarii* I–IV (Venice, 1578).

Wiesen, D. S., *St Jerome as a Satirist* (Ithaca and New York, 1964).

The Wife's Lament, ed. R. F. Leslie, in *Three Old English Elegies* (Manchester, 1961), pp. 47–48.

York Ritual, see under *Manuale . . . Eboracensis*.

Ywain and Gawain, ed. A. B. Friedman and N. T. Harrington, EETS, o.s. 254 (1964).

D Women and Letters

Abelard and Héloise, *The Letters of Abelard and Héloise*, trans. B. Radice (Harmondsworth, 1974).

Andreas Capellanus, *The Art of Courtly Love*, trans. J. J. Parry (New York, 1941).

Anselm, *Letters*, ed. F. S. Schmitt in *Anselmi Opera* IV and V (Edinburgh, 1946–61).

Atkinson Jenkins, see *Eructavit*.

Benton, J. F., 'The Court of Champagne as a Literary Center', *Speculum*, 36 (1961), 551–91.

Bernard of Clairvaux, *Sermones Super Cantica Canticorum*, ed. J. Leclerq o.s.b., C. H. Talbot, and H. M. Rochais o.s.b. in *Works* I and II (Rome, 1957–).

Bliss, see *Sir Launfal*.

Böddekker, K., 'Versifizirte Benediktinerregel im "Northern Dialect"', *Englische Studien*, 2 (1879), 60–93.

Butler, Sr. M. M., *Hrotswitha: The Theatricality of her Plays* (New York, 1960).

Catherine of Siena, *Dialogo* 'Dialogues', ed. I. Taurisano o.p. (Rome, 1947).

Catherine of Siena, *Letters*, ed. N. Tommaseo and P. Miscatelli, I–VI (Siena, 1913–21, and Florence, 1939–47).

Chrétien de Troyes, *Le Chevalier de la Charrete (Lancelot)*, ed. M. Roques (Paris, 1958).

Chrétien de Troyes, *Erec et Enide*, ed. W. Foerster (Halle, 1890); Textausgabe 1896 (3rd edn 1934).

Coulton, G. G., *Monastic Schools in the Middle Ages*, Medieval Studies, X (London, 1913).

Deanesly, M., 'Vernacular Books in England in the fourteenth and fifteenth centuries', *MLR*, 15 (1920), 349–58.

Denis Piramus, *La Vie Seint Edmund le Rei*, ed. H. Kjellman (Göteborg, 1935).

Dhuoda, *Manuel pour mon Fils*, ed. P. Riché, trans. B. de Vregille and C. Mondesert, SC CCXXV (1976).

Donaldson, E. T., *Speaking of Chaucer* (London, 1970).

Elisabeth of Schönau, *Liber Revelationum Elisabeth De Sacro Exercitu Virginum Coloniensium* 'Revelations on the Band of Holy Virgins of Cologne', in *Die Visionen und Briefe der Heil. Elisabeth sowie die Schriften Aebte Ekbert und Emecho von Schönau*, ed. F. W. E. Roth (Brünn, 1886), pp. 123–38.

Elisabeth of Schönau, *Liber Viarum Dei* 'On the Ways of God', in *Die Visionen und Briefe der Heil. Elisabeth sowie die Schriften Aebte Ekbert und Emecho von Schönau*, ed. F. W. E. Roth (Brünn, 1886), pp. 88–122.

Elisabeth of Schönau, *Visiones*, in *Die Visionen and Briefe der Heil. Elisabeth sowie die Schriften Aebte Ekbert und Emecho Von Schönau*, ed. F. W. E. Roth (Brünn, 1886), pp. 1–87.

Eructavit, an Old French metrical paraphrase of Psalm XLIV . . . Attributed to

Adam de Perseigne, ed. T. Atkinson Jenkins, *Gesellschaft für Romanische Literatur*, 20 (Dresden, 1909).

Fox, J. C., 'Marie de France', *EHR*, 25 (1910), 303–306, and 26 (1911), 317–26.

Frank, R. W. Jr., *Chaucer and the Legend of Good Women* (Cambridge, Mass., 1972).

Gertrud of Helfta, *Exercita Spiritualia* 'Les Exercices', trans. J. Hourlier and A. Schmitt, SC CXXVII, (1967).

Gertrud of Helfta, *Legatus Divinae Pietatis* 'Le Héraut: Memorial des Largesses de l'Amour Divin', trans. P. Doyère, SC CXXXIX and CXLIII, (1968).

Haight, A. L., ed. *Hroswitha of Gandersheim, Her Life, Time and Works* (New York, 1965).

Héloïse, see Abelard and Héloïse.

Hildegard of Bingen, *Epistolae*, in *Opera Omnia*, PL CXCVII, 145–382.

Hildegard of Bingen, *Physica*, Libri IX, in *Opera Omnia*, PL CXCVII, 1125–1352.

Hildegard of Bingen, *Scivias*, Libri III, in *Opera Omnia*, PL CXCVII, 383–738.

Holmes, U. T., *History of Old French Literature* (New York, 1937).

Hrotswitha, *The Plays of Roswitha*, trans. C. St John (London, 1923). See also Haight and Wiegend.

Julian(a), Anchoret of Norwich, *Revelations of Divine Love*, ed. G. Warrack, 13th edn (London, 1949).

Julian(a), Anchoret of Norwich, *Revelations of Divine Love*, trans. C. Wolters (Harmondsworth, 1966).

Kempe, Margery, *The Book of Margery Kempe*, trans. W. E. I. Butler-Bowden, introd. R. W. Chambers (London, 1936).

Kjellmann, see Denis Piramus.

Knighton, H., *Chronicon*, I–II, RS 92 (London, 1889 and 1895).

Knowles, D., *The Religious Orders in England* (Cambridge, 1955).

Lawlor, J., ed., *Patterns of Love and Courtesy* (London, 1966).

Lancelot, see Chrétien de Troyes, *Le Chevalier de la Charrete*.

Legge, M. D., *Anglo-Norman Literature and its Background* (Oxford, 1963).

Life of St Catherine, see Paris.

Loomis, R. S., *Arthurian Literature in the Middle Ages* (Oxford, 1959).

McLeod, E., *Héloïse* (London, 1938).

McLeod, E., *The Order of the Rose, The Life and Ideas of Christine de Pizan* (London, 1976).

Manly, J. M., ed., *The Canterbury Tales* (New York, 1928).

Mann, J., *Chaucer and Medieval Estates Satire* (Cambridge, 1973).

Marie de France, *Espurgatoire S. Patrice*, ed. K. Warnke, *Bibliotheca Romanica*, ix (Halle-an-der-Saale, 1938).

Marie de France, *Fables* (selected) ed. A. Ewert and R. C. Johnston (Oxford, 1942).

Marie de France, *Lais*, ed. A. Ewert (Oxford, 1944).

Mechthild of Hackeborn, *The Book of Gostlye Grace* (15th-cent. Eng. trans. of Mechthild's *Liber Specialis Gratiae*), ed. T. A. Halligan (Toronto, 1979).

Mechthild of Magdeburg, *The Revelations of Mechthild of Magdeburg* or *The Flowing Light of the Godhead*, trans. L. Menzies (London, 1953).

Mickel, E. J. Jnr., 'A Reconsideration of the *Lais* of Marie de France', *Speculum*, 46 (1971), 39–65.

Paris, G., 'La Vie de Sainte Catherine de Soeur Clémence de Barking', *Romania*, 13 (1884), 400–403.

Parry, see Andreas Capellanus.

Pernoud, R., *Héloise et Abelard* (Paris, 1970).

Pizan, Christine de, *Lavision-Christine*, ed. M. L. Towner (Washington, 1932).

Pizan, Christine de, *Le Livre du Chemin de longue estude*, ed. R. Püschel (Berlin, 1887, Repr. Geneva, 1974).

Pizan, Christine de, *Le Livre du Corps de Policie*, ed. R. H. Lucas (Geneva and Paris, 1967).

Pizan, Christine de, *Le Livre des fais et bonnes meurs de Charles V*, ed. S. Solente, I–II (Paris, 1936).

Pizan, Christine de, *Le Livre de la Mutacion de Fortune*, ed. S. Solente, I–IV (Paris, 1959–68).

Pizan, Christine de, *Le Livre de la Paix*, ed. C. C. Willard ('s Gravenhage, 1958).

Pizan, Christine de, *Oeuvres Poétiques*, ed. M. Roy, I–III, SATF (1886).

Power, E., *Medieval People* (New York, 1963).

Radice, see Abelard and Héloise.

Rajna, P., 'Tre Studi per la Storia del libro di Andrea Capellano', *Studj di Filologia Romanza*, 5 (1891), 193–272.

Riché, see Dhuoda.

Roy, see Pizan.

Rule of St Benedict (rhymed), see Böddekker.

Sir Launfal, ed. A. J. Bliss (London, 1960).

Solente, see Pizan.

Stevens, J., 'The *granz biens* of Marie de France', in *Patterns of Love and Courtesy* ed. J. Lawlor (London, 1966), pp. 1–25.

St John, see Hrotswitha.

Steadman, J. M., 'The Prioress's Dogs and the Benedictine Rule', *MP*, 54 (1956), 1–6.

Wiegend, Sr. M. G., *The Non-Dramatic Works of Hroswitha* (St Louis, Mo., 1936).

Wormald, C. P., 'The Uses of Literacy in Anglo-Saxon England and its Neighbours', *TRHS*, 5th Series, 27 (1977), 95–114.

E   *Conclusion*

Albertus Magnus, *Quaestiones Super de Animalibus*, ed. E. Filthaut o.p. in *Opera Omnia* XII (Aschendorf, 1955).

Aristotle, *Generation of Animals*, trans. A. L. Peck (London, 1943).

Aristotle, *Historia Animalium*, trans. A. L. Peck, I–II (London, 1965–70).

Bracton, H., *Note Book*, ed. F. W. Maitland, I–III (London, 1887).

Buckstaff, F. J., 'Married Women's Property in Anglo-Saxon and Anglo-Norman Law', *American Academy of Political and Social Sciences Annals*, 4 (1893), 233–64.

Bullough, V. L., 'Medieval and Scientific Views of Women', *Viator*, 4 (1973), 485–501.

Clark, C., 'Women's names in Post-Conquest England: Observations and Speculations', *Speculum*, 53 (1978), 223–51.

Glanvill, R., *De Legibus et Consuetudinibus Regni Anglie*, ed. G. D. G. Hall (London, 1967).

Haskell, A. S., 'The Portrayal of Women by Chaucer and His Age', in *What Manner of Woman*, ed. M. Springer (Oxford, 1977), pp. 1–14.

Judd, E., 'Women before the Conquest: a Study of Women in Anglo-Saxon England', *Papers in Women's Studies*, 1 (1974), 127–49.

Lydgate, J., *The Temple of Glas*, ed. J. Norton-Smith in *John Lydgate, Poems* (Oxford, 1966), pp. 67–112.

Lydgate, J., *Troy Book*, ed. H. Bergen, EETS, e.s. 97, 103, 106, 126 (1906–35, Repr. 1973).

McNamara, J. A., and Wemple, S. F., 'The Power of Women through the Family, in Medieval Europe 500–1100', *Feminist Studies*, 1 (1973), 126–41.

Mead, K. C. H., *A History of Women in Medicine* (Haddam, Conn., 1943).

Needham, J., *A History of Embryology* (New York, 1959).

Pollock, F., and Maitland, F. W., *History of English Law*, I–II (Cambridge, 1898, Repr. 1968).

Renoir, A., 'Attitudes towards Women in Lydgate's Poetry', *ES*, 42 (1961), 1–14.

Stenton, F. M., 'The Historical Bearing of Place Name Studies. The Place of Women in Anglo-Saxon Society', *TRHS*, 4th Series, 25 (1943), 1–13.

Stonor Letters And Papers 1290–1483, ed. C. L. Kingsford, Camden Society, 3rd Series 29–30 (London, 1919).

F *Further Reading*

Baker, D., (ed.), *Medieval Women*, SCH, Subsidia I (Oxford, 1978).

Hoecke, W. van, and Welkenhuysen, A., (eds.), *Love and Marriage in the Twelfth Century* (Louvain, 1981).

Ladurie, E. Le Roy, *Montaillou*, trans. B. Bray (Harmondsworth, 1980).

Le Menagier de Paris, ed. G. E. Brereton and J. M. Ferrier (Oxford, 1981).

Pernoud, R., *Aliénor d'Aquitaine* (Paris, 1965).

Pernoud, R., *La Femme au Temps des Cathédrales* (Paris, 1980).

Stuard, S. M., (ed.), *Women and Medieval Society* (Pennsylvania, 1976).

Sumption, J., *Pilgrimage* (London, 1975).

Index

INDEX